THE SOUL'S JOURNEY

To Jane,
your light is
tender cover, please
allow this book to awaken
your many talents to help others

Love
Lee

4/27/13

THE SOUL'S JOURNEY

REGRESSION CASES OF PARALLEL LIVES, ATTACHMENTS, LIGHT BEINGS, AND LOVE'S TRIUMPH

LEE MITCHELL

CASEY PUBLISHING
LITTLETON, CO

The Soul's Journey
Copyright © 2013 by Lee Mitchell

ISBN-13: 978-0-9889250-0-7

Printed in the United States of America
by Casey Publishing
Littleton, CO 80123

First Edition

Cover Design and Book Design by Maryann Brown

*The strong and courageous cheetah
on the cover represents all the big cats
that lovingly protect me and watch
over me at all times. Cheetah responds
to opportunity without hesitation
when it presents itself. And so I try to
do the same.*

Worn-out Garments
Are shed by the body:
Worn-out bodies
Are shed by the dweller
Within the body
New bodies are donned
By the dweller, like garments.

Not wounded by the weapons,
Not burned by the fire,
Not dried by the wind,
Not wetted by water:
Such is the Atman*,

Not dried, not wetted,
Not burned, not wounded,
Innermost element,
Everywhere, always,
Being of beings,
Changeless, eternal,
For ever and ever.

The Bhagavad-Gita

*the godhead within us all

Contents

PREFACE

I am meeting friends this week to celebrate 12/12/12. We are gathering with chants, drumming, and crystal bowls to send love and peace to our mother Earth. Through thoughts of this celebration, which will be coinciding with celebrations all over the world, I have come to realize that love and peace are the common themes of this book.

All of us want inner peace and love for ourselves and our loved ones. But these are very trying times for humans in the world. Americans are involved in two wars, we have had record natural disasters this year of flooding, hurricanes, and earthquakes, and our economic future in the U.S., Great Britain, Greece, Italy, France, and even Iceland seems uncertain at best. The hope for that peace and love seems very dim for many at this time in our history.

The stories you are about to read are concerning average human beings having very unusual spiritual experiences. Whether they want to bring back peace to their lives, and hope that looking at past life trauma can do that by releasing pent-up pain held onto for too long, or they want to bring peace and love back to their hearts through clear understanding of their present relationships by looking at past lives with these same soul partners. These relationships with members of their soul group have played out over centuries, life after life, as you will see revealed in the chapters coming up.

For some in these stories, they just had a life that seemed so very unsettling, that they came to past life therapy in hopes that they could ease their pain at feeling they don't belong here on earth. They hoped the altered state of their subconscious, while in trance, would give them some answers for peace, love and happiness in their present lives.

Probably the most confused and displaced clients looking for peace and love are the ones that are here for a mission from far, far away, but do not consciously remember what that mission is. They are searching for clarity and understanding for their role here and are looking for like-minded travelers who are warriors like themselves to enjoy their earthly existence while they fight the war to save planet Earth.

I hope that the participants in this book have been helped on their journey by the benefits they received in past life and spiritual soul regression therapy work with me. There are many other stories, just as important, that are not in this book, of people also looking for the peace and love in their present lives that we all seek. I believe that spiritual regression hypnotherapy is a tried and proven method for opening our hearts to expose old, painful traumas to shine the light on them once and for all, to dispel the darkness that has been associated with these traumas, and release them to ensure that love and peace can indeed be theirs for the taking. May these stories reach out to touch others, like the people in this book, to bring awareness to many that peace and love is available to us all.

Lee Mitchell   December 2012

ACKNOWLEDGEMENTS

This book could not have reached completion without the encouragement and work of many friends and professionals. I would like to thank Elizabeth Amigo, first, for her level of excellence in editing each and every page until they were just right. I know it was trying for you, Elizabeth. Thank you for having patience with me. Then my good friend, Marta Shoman, must be acknowledged for her professional critique. Marta forced me to look at the themes and ideas of the book before anyone else was allowed to see the first manuscript. Marta became that little teacher inside my head. Thank you, Marta.

My immense thanks to Liz Wendling, president of Sales Coach for Women in Denver. Just coincidently we became neighbors just when I started this book and she introduced me to many of the professionals below whom she had used and enjoyed. There are no coincidences, you know Liz. I have so enjoyed our walks with Casey and Hanna, our dogs, over all these many months.

My sincere thanks to Maryann Brown for her book formatting. She is a professional in all that she does. Thank you, Maryann, for not only putting the book in the correct format for book printing, but the beautiful, yet simple, design of the cover. Gail Nelson, my deepest appreciation for your skill in putting this book into e-book format. Amazon thanks you and I thank you for your experience in formatting in all forms of e-book organization. You make me and my book look progressive and current.

Many friends helped along the way to lift my spirits as deadline after deadline was not met. My thanks goes to my dear friends, Jeannine Lehman, Shaylene Wright, and Pat Opper. I also must mention my friend, Suzy Emmett, and her insight as a medium and psychic. Suzy encouraged me from the start to get this book out to the public to help others. I know all of you just wanted me to reach the finished product for my own satisfaction of completion. This book has been a goal of mine for many, many months. I also want to thank Margo Park. She was my mentor, though she is not a past life regression therapist. Margo helped me start my career of past life regression therapist and spiritual intuitive by guiding me in my first few months. Your light goes far, my friend.

I would also like to thank Linda Backman, PhD. and her husband Earl Backman who certified me in past life regression therapy. Also, Anne and Greg of the Association of Transpersonal Psychology & Hypnotherapy for certifying me in hypnotherapy, and Dr. Brian Weiss, MD, and Michael Newton PhD. for their influence in my education of past life and between life hypnotherapy.

Most importantly, I want to thank all the kind and sincere clients of past life regression sessions that are exhibited in this book. Without their stories, there would be no book to inform others. Thank you all so much for allowing me to bring your stories to light to inform and enlighten others of past life and between life therapy.

CHAPTER ONE:
INTRODUCTION

It takes courage to pursue the path of alignment with spirit and with your truest nature. The spiritual warrior in all of us is being called to action in these most chaotic and uncertain, yet exciting, times on our planet Earth.

As a Certified Past Life Regression Therapist and a spiritual intuitive, I work with many people who are searching for clarity regarding their soul's purpose. Many have strayed from their higher self's chosen path and are out of alignment with their soul's path. In the early 21st century, we are awakening to the use of multisensory tools in this self-discovery path. For many, it's unsettling to use such tools.

Yet, others embrace these new-found abilities of listening to their inner knowing, which is their highest self. People are being uplifted in listening to certain frequencies of music or tonal music, or resonating with the "I AM" mantras that open up enlightened corridors of their inner soul self. Some allow the interconnected feeling to expand into work with volunteer groups, or green-formed organizations, or spiritual pursuit groups that open their hearts and minds to their evolution.

As a part of the transition into this human soul-shift, we must investigate the dark recesses of our hearts and minds. The traumas and pains from the past can be found there in "the shadow" as described by a grandfather of psychology, Carl G. Jung. We must heal the past by facing the truth of our life experience. Take responsibility for the choices we made, face the pain, let go of guilt and accept that the past has had a profound impact on the present. The time has come to self-liberate, heal and set ourselves free. To want freedom from past hurts and to achieve this liberation are very different things. But the first step is to have the longing and courage to heal. Past life regression therapy is a very valid source for this healing.

Personal research and the development of clinical hypnosis techniques are helping clients to access their soul memories about past lives and the afterlife. Achieving a super-conscious trance state to recall one's memories of past lives and the soul's path trajectory is a major theme of this book. By safely re-experiencing the scenes of the traumatic experiences, and the emotional feelings that parallel these traumas, the client is freed to delete the shadow energy, and release it for good. These traumas will continue to affect our present lives if we do not uncover the emotion behind them. They trap us in a mesh of density that prevents us from more fully being in total alignment with spirit.

SPIRITUAL REGRESSION THERAPY IS A COMBINATION OF PAST LIFE REGRESSION THERAPY AND SPIRITUAL SOUL REGRESSION

Past life regression (PLR) therapy and between lives regression (BLR) hypnotherapy constitute spiritual regression therapy. The hypnosis facilitator should be well educated in the field of metaphysics in order to be able to analyze the karmic influences in a client's existence from both psychological and historical perspectives.

In past life regression therapy, the hypnotherapist is taking the client to a light alpha brain wave state to experience a past life or lives that will help them release emotions that are attached to trauma from these past lives in their present life. In between lives regression therapy, the hypnotherapist is taking the client to a deeper theta brain wave state to experience not only a most recent past life, but also to experience their soul state in a realm where they reside as spirit. The client meets their soul group, guided by their master guide, and also reviews their performance in this past life with their Council of Elders, and they meet specialty groups they work with in spirit. Depending on the client, other topics may be addressed in BLR, such as how many lives they have lived before their present one. Usually, a client will experience a PLR before journeying through a BLR.

Past life regression and between lives regression work can help open the doors of understanding. In regression hypnotherapy, any desired present life shift in thinking evolves from conscious and unconscious processes led by the client's higher self and their team of spiritual guides and teachers.

The comparison of living our lives on earth to being an actor who takes a role in a stage play can be a helpful analogy for understanding past life work. You may decide to be the female lead role in a life, and some of your soul group members may take the male lead role or the supporting role as best friend, the friend from college role, your children with you and your spouse, and so on. Our human bodies can be compared to the costumes an actor wears for his role in the play. The difference between a human soul and an actor in a play is that souls accumulate all the life experiences as they evolve in many lives, while actors simply drop the role and move on when the next role is offered. These life experiences can be positive ones that make us stronger or negative patterns and dependent traits that weaken us. Many times we will repeat patterns life after life.

As the Yogi, Paramahansa Yogananda, from **Autobiography of a Yogi**, so elegantly stated:

> "Do not take life's experiences too seriously. Above all, do not let them hurt you, for in Reality they are nothing but dream experiences. If circumstances are bad and you have to bear them, do not make them a part of yourself. Play your part in life, but never forget that it is only a role."
>
> *Paramahansa Yogananda*

Past life regression work can allow our higher superconscious to return to these traumatic events that set up the negative patterns, and help us release the emotion and spiritual attachment we have to them.

The positive life experiences allow us to strengthen our spiritual muscle in order to take on more complex roles here on earth. The more times we experience the pain of losing a loved one and triumph in spite of it, we are made stronger. The more we blossom from tragic and hard beginnings to a mature, competent adult, the more our souls strengthen. These are the ultimate qualities of confidence, compassion, and love of who we truly are at our core soul self.

21st CENTURY LEADERS IN PAST LIFE REGRESSION

The most recent beginning of past life regression therapy work was brought to public attention in the 1980s. Dr. Brian Weiss wrote his best-selling book, *Many Lives, Many Masters* in 1988. Publishing this landmark text resulted in his resignation from his commanding job as Chairman of Psychiatry at Mount Sinai Medical Center in Miami to practice past life regression hypnotherapy and lecture world-wide on the benefits of looking at past life events. He weighed his decision to leave traditional psychiatry for almost 10 years before coming out with this best-selling book. I personally followed the researcher, Dr. Michael Newton, when his books came out in the 1990s. Dr. Michael Newton is the 21st century psychologist and hypnotherapist who brought national attention to PLR with his thought-provoking books, *Journey of Souls* (1994) and *Destiny of Souls* (2000), which have been translated into over thirty languages. He is also the author who coined the phrase, Life Between Lives Regression. His insights are derived from personally facilitating over 7,000 clients into their spiritual life between physical incarnations on Earth.

More recently, Dolores Cannon has come forward with detailed documentation of past life regression therapy. Dolores Cannon is an international public speaker and author on past life regression. She has published over 20 volumes of interesting work including her best-selling series, *Convoluted Universe, Books 1 through 4.* Dolores Cannon has facilitated cases from all over the world as she lectures at her seminars. Now well into her 80s, she reports from clients whose souls have traveled to be on earth from other planets and galaxies. Dolores Cannon has now done thousands of regressions and has given her opinion on the validity of this research into our soul's past:

> It is a valuable tool, but that is all it is, a tool. When you begin to evolve and know yourself, then you no longer need to continue going back into the past. The past memories are good and valuable information, but they must be put to use in the present body, especially family relations. We have to weave it all together the same way we have woven the memories of our own childhood and other experiences.
>
> For good or bad, they are the story of our life and must be dealt with and reconciled. This helps make the individual a well-rounded and sane personality.[1]

A Rocky Mountain regional leader in past life regression is Greg McHugh, with his book, *The New Regression Therapy*. In this book, Greg explores his work with releasing attachments from our souls during past life regression hypnosis. And my certification teacher, Dr. Linda Backman, author of *Bringing Your Soul To Light*, studied and taught with Dr. Michael Newton. She co-created and served on the founding board of the Society for Spiritual Regression, now The Michael Newton Institute for LBL (life between lives) Hypnotherapy, in 2005 through 2006. This institute trains professionals to be facilitators of past life regression and LBL. Linda Backman says it best when she describes the benefits of PLR:

> Neither the client nor the therapist has complete control over the session. It is the client's team of guides and teachers in the unseen world who determine the content of the regression. Simply stated, regression hypnotherapy is a precise and powerful tool you can use to access and deepen your understanding of your core self. It can open a unique window on any number of issues and life circumstances.[2]

The 21st century is a time when metaphysics, spirituality, quantum physics, and brain science are merging on multiple levels. Recently, the Dalai Lama met with the

---

[1]Dolores Cannon, *Convoluted Universe, Volume 4,* (Huntsville, Arkansas: Ozark Mountain Publishing, 2012), 4.

[2]Linda Backman, Ph.D., *Bringing Your Soul to Light, HealingThrough Past Lives me Between,* (Woodbury, Minnesota: Llewellyn Publications, 2009), 3.

Mind Life Institute to discuss spirituality's role in the study of the mind. Dr. Mehmet Oz on his new medical show, *Dr. Oz*, frequently brings on alternative health professionals such as acupuncture, massage, and psychic leaders to discuss their roles in the mind, body, and spirit connection.

BASIC BRAIN SCIENCE

To give you some technical background on past life regression therapy, here is the list of the brain wave states that are addressed in hypnotherapy.

1. Beta state is a full-awake conscious state.
2. Alpha states involve light, medium, and deeper trance levels.
   a. The lighter stages are typically those we use for meditation.
   b. The medium stages are generally associated with recovering childhood memories and past trauma. These stages are useful for behavior modification such as quitting smoking or gaining/losing weight.
   c. The alpha states involve past life recovery.
3. The theta state is as deep as we get before losing consciousness, and it uncovers the area of the super-conscious mind that reveals our spiritual life between lives activity.
4. The delta state is our final deep sleep state.

There are major distinctions between PLR and BLR. A past life regression begins with a simple induction process that relaxes the client and moves the brain from waking beta brain waves to a creative and restful alpha brain wave state. It's a light trance and opens up the connection to the subconscious. Clients are taken to the theta brain wave, a state of deeper relaxation, in the between lives regression.

It is in the theta brain wave state that the client connects to the higher soul self. This is the dimension where we view our Council of Elders, our original soul group, have a review of soul's trajectory, visit the specialty soul groups we work with, and much more. This is to name just a few of the events you will experience in a between lives soul regression.

MY OWN SOUL REGRESSION BEGINS THE JOURNEY

In discussing the benefits of past life regression, I work with clients to overcome many life challenges. The most common challenges are relationship traumas, health issues, phobias, grieving, karmic situations, career choices, and emotions.

This book is a compilation of case studies beginning with a regression from my own life. My father, Winston, and mother had four children; my sister, myself the middle child, and my two younger brothers. When I was four, my father and mother divorced. During my elementary and middle school years, my mother struggled to support us children on a high school education. My father failed to give her child support and we rarely saw him. I remember telling myself that I would never be like my mother. I would get an education and I would have a career before I started a family. I had experienced my mother's sadness in losing a husband that she truly loved. When I was fourteen, my mother died of complications from asthma. Fortunately, I was able to go live with my grandmother, whom I was very close to. My two brothers were shuffled off to live with my sister and her husband.

Over my adult years, I remember working very hard to forgive Winston, who passed on while I was in my twenties. I wrote letters to him, which I never mailed, forgiving him. I told myself that he was just human and he made choices he thought were best for everyone involved. Still, there was a part of myself that held a small remnant of anger and resentment toward Winston. I needed to release this anger and resentment to move beyond the last remaining emotional trauma and come to a new feeling of forgiveness and love for Winston.

I experienced a couple of past life regressions years ago in Crestone, Colorado. This was to expressly look at lives with the soul of Winston. One I experienced showed me as a weeping woman in her forties. He was a much younger man in his twenties. He was also weeping in the scene. We were standing in a cave and we were saying goodbye to each other. We were lovers and we were letting go of each other. The time period was the Middle Ages, sometime in the 1400s. At my age, it was not proper for us to be lovers. I doubt that I could still bear children. We both knew we would never be accepted into our village. We knew he was leaving to go off to war. We both knew that we would probably never see each other again. So the young man (Winston) was leaving for the war to save my reputation. In the final scene I saw, he was separated from his group in the army. I knew that he essentially starved to death on a mountaintop, looking for food.

I was to see this past life to help me understand that Winston did not have the tools to be a responsible father or husband because he had given all that up and died early. As a result of my regression, I understood that the soul of Winston in this present life, as my father, held fears based on his past lives.

Moving forward to the present, I had a session with medium Michelle Moceri. In the session, Michelle was able to connect with Winston, my mother and my grandmother in spirit. The first connection Michelle saw was Winston on his knees with his palms together and open toward me. He said through Michelle, "Tell my daughter, I am sorry, I am so sorry. I apologize for not being there for her." I asked

Winston, through Michelle, "Why did you leave Mother with four young children?"

His response was, "There are no excuses for my actions, but my upbringing was pretty grim, and I was in no position to be a father, let alone a husband. Yet, I know there is no excuse for what I did to you and the family." I resigned myself that that was the conclusion of his insight to his life with us. At the end of the session, Michelle said that Winston had one final thing for me that was very important before they pulled their energy away. She communicated for Winston: "Our life with you was a soul contract. Your mother and I left you early in your youth to ensure your soul's path. You had to mature quickly and be very independent at a young age because you had chosen a path of singleness and purpose." This statement really made me reflect on my growing up and taking on life as an adult.

I moved through careers as a clothing buyer, general contractor in residential homes, and real estate broker, always searching for "my calling." Intuition told me to pursue training in past life regression in 2007. I enrolled in a certification class with Dr. Linda Backman. I learned much from her and Dr. Michael Newton's techniques that I use today. And this work does take a tremendous amount of soul strength and confidence in one's approach with clients. The greatest gift my parents gave me was the difficult opportunity of growing up in a non-traditional environment.

The traumatic losses that humans experience are to serve as the foundation for becoming free thinkers and self-sufficient in our adult lives. If I urge my clients to take trauma experiences that they view in past lives as growth experiences for their soul and to accept them as a gift, then I most certainly must accept this knowledge from my father in the same vein. Just as I accept my father's role in my life, I urge my clients to do the same.

If you are reading this book, you are a light worker, spiritual warrior, and evolved soul who can use this book to unlock the blockages within your current life in order to realize your soul's purpose in the now. In the chapters ahead, you will experience past life cases that you may identify with or see in others. We are all here to be students and teachers for each other at this time of oneness.

CHAPTER TWO
TRAUMATIC RELATIONSHIPS UNDERSTOOD

Inner peace can be reached
Only when we practice forgiveness.
Forgiveness is the letting go of the past,
And is therefore the means for correcting
Our misperceptions.
> *Gerald G. Jampolsky*
> *Love is Letting Go of Fear*

The most common reason a client will request a past life regression is to discover why personal relationships are not successful, happy or rewarding for them. The emotional scars from fears, physical and verbal abuse, and insecurities come from our most intimate relationships in present and past lives. Male clients' emotional trauma generally comes from relationships involving events. These events could be wars, battles, or destruction within the family. The running theme for female clients concerns their male relationships. Their interactions with husbands, fathers, sons, and other male partners in past lives needs to be re-experienced to finally "delete" the misperceptions or traumas in order to enjoy healthy relationships in the present life.

Susan was just such a client. The first past life regression question that she wanted to explore was, "Why do I have such difficulties in all my male relationships?" Before the regression, we discussed her history, including the relationship with her father, Ron. She revealed to me that Ron had recently passed. His death deeply upset her, yet she was grateful for some quality time with her father before he passed.

Susan told me that her father, Ron, had been physically abusive to her all her young life while she was growing up with several siblings. He seemed to pick on her only and make her the scapegoat for many of the family troubles. She did, however, feel the two had been able to put closure on this history of abuse in their relationship before his death.

As we begin the past life regression, Susan goes into trance easily and starts describing what she sees in the past life.

S: It's smoky, but I see forty-foot-high rock walls before me. They are surrounding a castle. I live there.

L: I ask her to describe how she is dressed and what she looks like.

S: I see that I am barefoot, and I have on a long white gown. I have long brown hair. My name is Aria and I am in my twenties.

L: I ask where she is living and what year it is.

S: I am in Scotland and the year is 1813.

L: I go back to her scene and ask her to describe her surroundings.

S: I am in my room. I see a really big, high-backed chair and a fireplace burning with smoke coming from it. (Why she saw smoke earlier.) I see high small windows are before me in the room. I feel terribly alone.

L: Next, I ask her about her parents.

S: They must be away. I don't see them and I am an only
     child. I feel sad. I am afraid as well. There is a lot of
     death around me as there is a war going on. I want to
     go hide in my bed. I want the servants to come in and
     tell me what is going on. Next, I see myself in bed with
     my knees pulled up with the covers around me. I am
     looking at the door. I hear movement outside my room.
     I am afraid. Yet, everyone (the servants) is running
     round inside the castle.

L: I ask about her mother.

S: My mother is not alive. That is why I am afraid. I have
     been alone for a long time. My father is away fighting,
     but he left the servants in charge to take care of me.
     Now the servants are coming in and taking me away.
     One is stern. An older woman. She's very pushy.

L: I ask Susan if she recognizes the woman's soul as anyone
     she would know in her present life.

S: It is my mother, Kay. The older woman servant is trying
     to get me to leave the castle. I am asking questions and
     she is trying to get me out. Now, I see other servants
     putting things away. They are trying to hide and protect
     the valuables from being stolen by the marauding
     armies on their way. The carriages are outside now.
     The dogs are there, too. One dog goes with me. I see
     that he is "Tusk." (Tusk is a dog that Susan had when
     she was younger.) We get in and drive off and it is a
     very bumpy road. I am not sure where we are going.
     There are two men driving the carriage. I cannot see
     out the carriage. It's cold and all I know is that I am
     being sheltered from the outside as we travel north.

I know that my father is angry. But I didn't do anything to make him angry.

L: I ask if Susan recognizes her father as anyone she knows in her current life.

S: I recognize my father as my present father, Ron.

L: Do you know your father's name in this past life?

S: My father's name is Herbert.

S: Now I see that as we travel, I start to see a lake on the right. I can feel the coolness from the water. It's early fall, August 18th. Then I see the carriage stopping. I can smell the hay and I see a fireplace burning. I see that it's my grandmother's home. I am very tired. We get out and get something to eat at my grandmother's place.

L: Do you recognize your grandmother's soul essence as anyone you recognize in your current life?

S: I see that the soul essence of the grandmother is my sister, Christine. I know that my grandmother knows something but won't tell me. The opposing army is taking over. I think that my father has been killed. My grandmother is telling me that I will be okay. The dog is barking and I know that my grandmother is ill and cannot go with us at this time as we leave to continue on our journey. Someone has arrived at my grandmother's. She brings gifts. My grandmother knew this person was coming to tell us that her son had been killed. The opposing army is the English Army. I'm afraid. They are telling us we are safe for a while, but more men, soldiers, are coming. Now I see that we are back in the carriages. We are going to France and we are crossing the water up north to get into France. My father was a general. He led a lot of men. A lot of men feared him. Wherever we stop for the night, I go upstairs to sleep. I feel numb and tired.

L: What is happening now? Lead us to the next most important scene.

S: Next morning, I hear a lot of movement. It's daylight, and there is talk of a boat. I am getting dressed in layers for the trip. We are now heading to the boat. It is very large and it smells. My grandmother and I are both there and we get on. The dog gets to go with us. We are saying goodbye to the carriage staff. It's a long trip. We land at Iceland or Greenland. There are allies there who will let us stay. The trip is very hard on Grandma. After we landed, it begins to snow. My grandmother gets out of the carriage and goes no farther. But I don't get to stay. They continue to take me on to a small village. There is a lodge in the middle of the village. There are little huts around the lodge. And a couple of servants who are now bringing me to meet an older man. His name is Eric and he is the leader of the village.

L: I ask Susan if she recognizes the soul essence of Eric as anyone she knows in her current life.

S: Susan recognizes Eric as her father Ron's best friend, Ormis. I see Eric as big and scary, but kind. I am given to him in marriage. They bring my grandma to me to live with us.....It's dirty. I don't like it there. I feel like I have lost everyone. I live my life out with him. I have a son.

L: I ask if she recognizes the soul essence of her son as anyone she knows in her current life.

S: My son is Mike in my present life. He is new in my life and I am presently dating him. (Mike had been one of the men she had asked about concerning her relationships and why she cannot have successful ones with men.)

L: I now ask Susan to move further in this past life on the count of three.

S: I see that my son is grown. He is handsome. Eric, my husband, has long ago died. I am now 45 years old. I'm saying goodbye to my son. I am dying. I'm old and sick. He is upset. We were very close.

L: I now move Susan's higher soul self away from that life and ask that her spirit guides come through to help us understand what she just experienced.

S: I see my master guide as strong, wise and courageous. His name is Trevor. He says, "You have gone through this a lot." In this past life I just experienced, I needed to learn how to adapt to change, to grow, and to love without control.

L: I ask her master guide, Trevor: "How does seeing this past life help Susan today?"

S: He says, through Susan, "Love is given to us as a gift. If we seek it or try to possess it, we cannot contain it. That is what Susan has been doing in her present life. If she will just allow, love will come. Relax. Do not treat loving like a job."

L: I ask Susan if there are any other guides that would like to come through. Many times to the left or right of the master guide we will see another force.

S: Yes, to the right of the master guide is another guide. It's bright, its essence is happy. It wants to be called Jolly. It is smaller than Trevor. Trevor looks like a big tree. He feels protective, kind, and loyal.

L: I ask Susan's guides about her life's path.

S: They say I'm not tapping into some ability I have. I'm not believing in myself. People are sent to me for healing. I am supposed to be bringing healing and joy to others. (Susan asks her spirit guides,) "What are the changes I need to make to reach my soul's work in this lifetime?" They are laughing, she says. I take things too seriously, and I give too much of myself. I am better when I am my goofy self. The guides say stop trying to be perfect. I am perfect just the way I am. By being goofy and lighthearted, I help people to open up to me. (Susan's spirit guides state more about her path.) I am not supposed to be building the world, I am supposed to be building people. (This is in reference to her current job, which is dealing with national companies in a sales capacity.) They say they have been sending messages, and I have been misinterpreting them. They say to become light and be present. I overcame the seriousness in the past life I just visited, but I am not doing the same in my present life. I have the power to build people, not to build things, because I feel people's soul essence. My gift of writing, and my gift of discernment is to be used to help others to find light and peace.

These PLR sessions showed several past lives with important men in Susan's present life today. Her spirit guides want her to understand the deeper meaning of why she needs to work through these hardships today with these men. We probably did not experience all the lives that Susan shared with these same men.

However, we were shown lives that helped her understand why the relationships are so tumultuous in her present life. Now the lesson for Susan and all female clients is to release the past life hurt, realizing it does not belong to the present life, and start to more fully enjoy and appreciate the relationships with these men today in the present under completely different circumstances and with different goals.

SPIRIT GUIDES AND TEACHERS

Spirit guides and teachers play a very important role in each past life regression. Along with the facilitator and the client, the spirit guides bring to the process the connection with the higher soul self. The soul level is where the core of our being resides. Any desired change in the present life stems from both conscious and unconscious processes led by the client's higher self and their team of spiritual guides and teachers.

Each client is different. Your spirit guides, along with your higher soul self, are the energy that brings you the past life. Whatever is important for you to experience for your soul's growth and understanding is what they will show you. Most people see past lives just as they would see scenes in a very detailed dream. Some are quickly whisked away by their guides to see prior civilizations their soul has been involved in, not necessarily on planet earth. Some have involved consultations with master guides and other ascended beings about their soul's path. All the experience is enlightening to your present life.

After the initial past life regressions, Susan consulted with me to help her pursue clearer understanding of her male relationships. After our initial sessions, Susan asked for coaching with her current relationship with Mike, who was the soul essence who was identified as her son in the life in Iceland. The two were slowly developing a friendship. She began to relax and let the love develop between them. "Instead of seeking to possess it, treat it like a gift" was her guides' suggestion. In March of 2012, Susan asked to start a series of past life regressions to investigate more fully this continued theme of her relationships with men. As we began the first session, she easily went into a light trance and as I asked her to open the door to a significant scene in an important past life, she relayed the following scene:

S: I am outside. There are a lot of people and buildings. We are in a marketplace. The year is 129 B.C. It is a very rich, and luxurious scene. It is Rome, Italy. It's a seaside location. I have on open-toed sandals, a long sheath, lots of jewelry, and I have a wig on. My sheath is off- white and tied in the middle. My name is Beratrue. I am busy talking and going through the crowds on my way somewhere. I am well known and older. I am in my 30's. Now I am walking down steps into grass. I am far away from the bustling marketplace. I am being pulled to the right. In front of me I see a cottage. I go in and there is another woman there. Her name is Lee Ann and she is a client and a friend.

L: I ask Susan if she recognizes the soul essence of the woman as anyone in her current life.

S: I recognize her as my friend, Lois.

L: What is happening now?

S: Lee Ann is excited about her daughter's upcoming wedding. I am helping with the preparation for the wedding and the future husband.

L: Once again, I ask Susan if she recognizes the daughter getting married as anyone she knows in her present life.

S: Yes, I recognize her as my friend Lois's daughter, Becky, today.

S: We are talking about the festivities and the dress I am making for the daughter. I am a seamstress. I make garments for the wealthy people and help them special occasion preparations.

L: I ask Susan to move to the next most important scene in this past life she is experiencing.

S: Lee Ann gives me (Beratrue) materials to take with me. I leave to go up towards the village again by a different path. I notice I pass an orchard, maybe an olive orchard as I go up a hill outside the eastern side of town. I see a nice house that I live in. I have a daughter, age 10, and her name is Anna. I have a son, age 9, and his name is Troy. I am telling Anna about the wedding plans. We are excited because she helps me with the dress. My husband is out. I am expecting him soon. His name sounds like Beau.

L: I ask Susan if she could identify the soul essence of her husband as anyone in her life today.

S: I see that his soul essence is my dad, Ron, in my present life.

S: I start preparing dinner and I call Troy to come inside to eat. My husband comes home and he is tired and doesn't want to hear anything from me about the day. He uses his mind at work. Later, he needs to go out for a while. I don't feel good about his leaving. He is close to our daughter, Anna. Now, I am getting the kids to bed. I am still upset with my husband for being out and leaving us alone. He does this often. He is seeing someone. I'm going to bed. He is still not home. Next morning I am up making breakfast and I see that my husband is there. The kids are getting eggs and milk from the chickens and goats outside. I try talking to Beau to remind him about an event coming up soon that we are to attend. I believe it's the wedding. He doesn't want to go. I know his mistress. Her name is Ray Anne. She is married, too. But I see myself cleaning up from breakfast and starting to work on the wedding dress. The kids are playing outside with the pet sheep. Then I hear someone come to the door. He is a man but his energy feels like a woman. It's Aaron. I greet him with a hug and a kiss. He is a man I have affection for.

L: I ask Susan if she recognizes Aaron as anyone in her current life.

S: I recognize him as my brother today.

S: Aaron lives close by. He is a friend. He is younger. He is sneaking away from work to see me because he really cares for me. Now I see that he is leaving because he has to get back to work. It's drudgery for him at work. He says be careful and that he cares for me.

L: I now ask Susan to move to the next most important scene on the count of three.

S: It is early evening. There is a party with music and elaborate food. It's the wedding. Everyone is jolly. I look behind the trees and I see my husband with Ray Anne embracing. I am looking for the bride. I am hugging her now. I now see a man but I am not going to approach him. I am really attracted to him. His name is Alex.

L: I ask Susan if she recognizes the soul essence of Alex as anyone she knows in her life today.

S: I recognize his soul essence as Keith, my longtime boyfriend of 11 years. I left him in California after I discovered him cheating on me.

L: Alex is a Roman soldier. He doesn't recognize me and I feel he doesn't know I care about him. Next, I see that my husband walks up to me. He takes me by the arm and tells me to gather the kids and go home. He is staying. I do it promptly. I am gathering the kids to leave. I say goodbye. I like the bride's new husband.

L: I ask if she recognizes the new husband as anyone she knows in her life today.

S: I recognize him as my pastor Ricky in my present life.

S: There are guards going to escort us home.

L: I ask Susan to move to the next most important scene.

S: I am in Alex's arms. I am kissing him. He does like me. Someone comes to the door. He is coming for both of us. I know the soldier. He is taking us. Something happened. Alex killed my husband! I am in shock. I didn't know.

Alex didn't like the way my husband treated me. He abused me. The guards have now separated us. I am asking about my kids. My husband was very controlling. He knew about Alex and me. We were having an affair. Now, they have taken me to a stone cell room alone. My son can't do anything to help me. My daughter will not come. She's angry at me. I am being led into a room with a dirt floor. There are people and guards around. Alex is there. It's like a trial. The guard I know is there. He turned us in. They are executing us! The guard just slit Alex's throat! They light me on fire! Then the same guard runs a sword through me. Our souls rise above the scene. I feel that this was unjust. I was set up. There was more going on behind the scene to this plot. My husband was in trouble. It was a political decision to get him killed. The guard was also angry. He wanted to see me fall. That is why he killed Alex first; to see me suffer. My husband knew things. He was like a spy. He was passing government secrets. A lot of people wanted him dead.

L: Can you identify the soul essence of the guard, Susan? It's important.

S: The guard is Mike, the man I am dating in my present life. I think he had a crush on me as the guard. He felt protective. He was angry with fear and jealousy. He desired me. He was angry that I took Alex over him. I never noticed him. Now, the guard feels bad that he caused this. Later, he drove himself crazy over what he had done in killing me and Alex in that past life.

L: Susan, ask for your spirit guides to come in and shed more light on why you were shown this past life. Susan sees the color of her guides: She sees purple, yellow and

green. Eric, her master guide, is here and he is smiling.
She says he is a great tree filled with kindness. Another
guide she sees is purple and his personality is happy and
goofy. Next, she sees Dawn, who is a loving guide but a
prankster. She is yellow and warm and compassionate.
Finally, Fred, who is loving, sweet happiness.

S: Please expand on the past life I just experienced. The
      spirit guides say that true love is loving, beyond and
      in spite of what we see. Compassion is the strongest
      emotion.

S: My guides are helping me to be compassionate. To make
      my own decisions and not have someone else do it for
      me. The lesson was all about forgiveness, even though
      they hurt me. My spirit guides say things between Mike
      (guard) and me are not over in this life. It's been many
      lifetimes since we have been together.

L: I ask the guides to give her help on her path, and Susan
      is told that being at peace and finding happiness is her
      goal in this life.

S: My spirit guides tell me I block my intuitive skills. I
      am supposed to be using them more in my current life
      path. My guides say they are always with me. I have
      completed things with Keith (Alex). I have not with
      my father (husband). We have ended our relationship
      in this current life as Susan on peaceful terms, but my
      guides say we will be together again. It will be a happy
      experience next time.

S: Everything is up in the air with Mike (guard), they say.
      He is a tight ball with a protective coating around him
      in this life. My guides say he has to have an emotional

breakthrough. He has to do it on his own. I am supposed
to wait.

In both past lives, Susan's father played a distant, cold
and even abusive role in her life. He did this, yet she was
able to forgive him in her present life before he died. He was
able to tell her was sorry as well. The separation between
her current boyfriend, Mike (guard), and Susan has been
going on for several months in this new year of 2012. He
keeps her on the outer realms of his personal life.

After the last regression, some new events have occurred.
Susan is venturing into a new business for herself. She will
be consulting clients in organization and planning space in
their homes and offices. She hopes to have the business up
and running by 2013. She feels Mike will be called on to help
her at times because he has building expertise that she will
need. Maybe he will let the walls down and forgive himself
for the guilt his higher consciousness feels for his actions in
the past life in Rome that prevents him from a relationship
with Susan. She feels this loving connection between Mike
and herself so strongly that she is unable to walk away. She
believes that her higher self is holding her in the relationship
with Mike. She is not to move on until a connection with Mike
is complete. As revealed in this series of regressions, Susan
and Mike have a soul contract to complete in the present life
and the relationship is not over for either one of them.

These past life cases show us that the dynamics between
souls may last life after life to complete a soul contract we
have with another. If we have unexplained feelings for
someone in our present life, it helps to look at the bigger
picture of past lives to explain the journey these two souls
may be on. Many times it cannot be explained or completed
in just this one present life. We all must keep working

through our problems with others, or they will just come through again in a future life. Dealing with hard issues with husbands, fathers, or sons will free women to complete their soul's path.

CHAPTER THREE
ATTACHMENTS FROM PAST LIVES THAT CAUSE NIGHTMARES

Many times the traumas incurred in past lives will not let us go. They "bleed" through into our present lives. Unless we investigate and resolve the emotional effects from the past that influence our current life, we will continue to suffer heartache, pain, and emotional distress. One such case that I worked with on attachments was shown by the spirit guides of the client during the regression why the attachments were haunting her. The client had connections to a friend from a past life that caused her great pain after his death. She also experienced the spirit world reaching out to her.

These traumas can arise from attachments that are spirits on the other side who need energy to stay connected to earth. These spirits can be harmless, but they do take your energy to support their staying on the earth plane. They can be shown the light in order to join their loved ones and release their earthbound energy once and for all. There are also attachments that can hold dark energy. These are dark energies that need to be released from the attachment and carried to the light source by light beings or angels of light. I work with both attachments with the help of my spirit guides who are ascended beings from the Great White Brotherhood (more about the Great White Brotherhood in Chapter Seven.) They help release the attachments by working with the Christ consciousness light.

Anne, my client, was to discover her soul's path when her spirit guides spoke to her in the past life regression session. Anne experienced spirit connection from the other side in the form of attachments to her spirit. She had become so frightened by their intervention into her daily life that she brought her husband into her dilemma to help her. In her dreams she was shouting out names and calling on the attachments. He would hold her and help her wake up from the bad dreams she would have.

In November of 2011, Anne and her husband came to me for help. The nightmares had continued for Anne Mendelson. She was also having severe headaches now as well. She had been to medical doctors for the headaches, and nothing seemed to be relieving her pain. As an army enlisted infantryman, Anne had just returned from a tour in Afghanistan nine months prior to our meeting. She had lost a close friend, James, whom she had met in boot camp. He had been killed in a bombing in Afghanistan. She had been devastated by his death. As a result, she had been unable to go to his burial site to say goodbye. She thought maybe the stress of losing her friend had something to do with the headaches and nightmares.

In addition, she and her husband had just welcomed their first child, a little girl. Anne worked part time and found life extremely difficult. As a last resort, she came to me to see if I could relieve the nightmares which prevented her from sleeping. Her husband said she would talk in her sleep in great distress from her dreams.

Her nightmares were of Native Americans and other figures following her. It appeared that they were stalking her in her nightmares, over and over. She simply did not understand why they were stalking her. Why did they want her attention?

In recent years, I have noticed that when a client's spirit guides want to make a clear and forceful point, they will show the client several lives in succession. When I first began doing past life regression work, this was not the case. Only occasionally would the client experience more than one life at a sitting. This is occurring now because of the quickening of our vibrational evolution and the shift of the earth's vibration as well. We are calling this the "Ascension." It is a shift in the human vibrational rate as we move from a carbon-based form to a crystalline-based form of energy. Our spirit guides know there is no time for clients to waste. They urgently want enlightenment for their clients. By showing several lives with similar themes, the client understands the message clearly. They may begin to make changes in their present lives to heal wounds caused from these past lives.

Such was the case with Anne Mendelson. Her spirit guides, teachers and her higher self led her through four lives. During the relaxation induction of the PLR, she imagined herself walking down a staircase and entering the hallway. I then asked her to stop at one particular door her guides have led her to so that she can enter a significant scene in a significant past life to explain her nightmares.

This is where our session begins.

L: As you enter the space, once you've opened the door, what do you see, Anne?

A: Wood structures on the ceiling. Outside I see a porch. I am in a log home. (The wood structures on the ceiling are probably wood beams used for support.)

L: Can you describe your clothing for me?

A: I have on flimsy slippers, a dress with buttons up the front.

L: Petend you put a mirror in front of your face and describe any details you see.

A: My hair is long and pulled up. My hair is red and my skin is pale.

L: How old do you look?

A: I am 30 years old.

L: What year is it? What is the first number that comes to your mind?

A: It is the West and the year is 1860.

L: Do you have children?

A: No children.

L: Are you married?

A:Y   es, my husband is Ben and he is in his 40s.

L: What is your name?

A: My name is Anna and I feel alone. Ben is working and he's been gone a long time. He's in the military.

L: Do you recognize the soul essence of your husband Ben as anyone you know in your present life as Anne?

A: Yes, he is my husband today.

L: I now ask Anne if we can move to the next most important scene in this past life she is currently looking at on the count of three.

A: Okay.

A: There are many people gathering. We are celebrating. I'm older. I'm 35 years old.

L: Do you have parents? (Many times parents are in our soul group and return many times with us.)

A: I have a father. My mother is not here. I have cousins. I recognize one cousin as a good friend, Sarah, that I work with at the jewelry store today in my present life. She is the female cousin in this past life. My father is not speaking to me. He's unhappy that my husband and I have not had children, considering how old I am……

A: I have really not wanted any children. In not having Ben around very much, I do not want children to take my attention away when he is here. I want to spend any time he is with me alone, just the two of us.

L: Let's now move forward in this past life to a point where both Anna and Ben are older on the count of three.

A: Ben has died. He's 78. We are burying him. I'm 63. I see friends and neighbors here to say goodbye. I recognize one neighbor as someone I know in my present life but cannot come up with the name in my mind. I am very upset over my husband dying. I cannot live without him. I see that I hang myself in our barn shortly after his death.

L: Anne, pull your soul essence away from the body of Anna now. As you rise and float up slowly, look back at the barn scene. Is there anyone in that life you would like to say goodbye to, to put closure to Anna's life?

A: Yes, my father. I am sorry I disappointed him.

Father: You never disappointed me, dear. (Her father is Anne's father in her current life, she later told me.)

I could tell this past life had come very quickly. That the ending had happened almost before the life scenes had begun. That is always a sign from the client's spirit guides to look at multiple past lives for deeper understanding.

L: Anne, I now want you to walk through a peaceful meadow. Next, as you step into a train tunnel, notice the opening at the end. I am going to count from ten down to one and when you reach one, you will be at the light opening at the far end of tunnel. Then, you will step out of the tunnel, into the light and into a significant past life.

A: It's daytime and I am outside. I see trees. Now, I see that there is something beyond the trees. I can't see what it is.

L: Please describe what clothing you are wearing.

A: I have on boots, pants, a jacket that buttons up. I have short hair. It's straight and dark.

L: How old do you look?

A: I'm in my 40s.

L: What is your name? First name that pops into your mind.

A: Adrian. The scene is somewhere in Europe. I think it's Germany.

L: What is the year?

A: It's sometime in the 1700s. As I get closer, now I can see by the trees that there is a tent. It's a big tent that you can sleep in. There is a man inside and he's angry. He's yelling. I feel there is a lot of tension. The man and I start shoving each other. I just broke his neck! I grab him and keep shoving.....When I looked down at his neck, it was disfigured.... I wanted to do this. I am getting the message that we were partners and we stole money. He then stole some of my share from me; my take. I am gathering the belongings. I left him underneath the remainder of the tent. I have the belongings and I am walking through the trees. No one is after me that I know.

A: Next, I see a wooden bridge. I walk over it and it breaks. It has rotting planks. The planks break and I fall. I stab myself with the planks. They stab me in the solar plexis. The fall kills me.

Once again, the message of this past life was clear and showed her a crucial past life death that her soul needed to re-experience to fully release the trauma behind it. The regression continues as I am directed to take Anne to another past life by my spirit guides.

L: I now want you to envision your soul floating among the clouds, Anne. The sky is blue and it's peaceful. Now imagine you drift down to a beautiful meadow with a soft gentle breeze blowing the grass gently. Anne, tell me what you are experiencing now.

A: It's evening. I am outside. I am in the middle of a war. There is a battle going on. It's the 1400s.

L: Do you get a sense of what country you are in?

A: It's Spain. I have black armor on. There is lots of
      fighting. I have a sword and a shield in my hands. There
      is a lot of chaos. I was ordered to keep fighting. My
      friend dies next to me. He was stabbed.

L: Do you recognize the soul essence of your friend as
      anyone you know in your present life?

A: Yes, my friend is James. (James is her friend from Boot
      Camp that was recently killed in Afghanistan.)

A: I have to continue because of all the chaos. There are
      a lot of dead bodies. There is a lot of blood. I go back
      to try to find my friend's body. His name is Stephan.
      I can't find him. I can't find him to bury him. I start
      digging graves for the others. There are so many, we
      are told to just burn them. We had to do it! I am in this
      constant grieving. It's because I didn't give Stephan a
      proper burial. A lot of people are getting sick now.

A: We are traveling to the next site. There are a few
      hundred of us left. We are all tired and sick. We have
      what's left of the food. I have a pain in my knee. I was
      injured in the last battle.

A: I have a pain in that knee today in my present life. I
      get an infection in the wound. They are talking about
      amputation. I don't want an amputation, but they take
      it anyway. I don't feel the pain any more. I go home to
      live with my mother. I help Mom with her bakery. I feel
      like I just lost my life as a soldier. ......I start debating
      with myself. I don't want to live. I love my Mother,
      but......

L: Do you recognize the soul essence of your mother as anyone you know in your present life?

A: She is my father, David, in my present life. Next, I see that on crutches, I take a walk toward a stone bridge with a pretty river running below it. I was never taught to swim. So, I see myself just rolling over the bridge, and I land in the water below. I simply fell over the bridge and I drown. It's cold. It takes very little time for me to die.

L: Please pull your soul's essence away from the body and rise above it. Looking down at the scene, is there anyone you would like to say goodbye to in order to put closure to that life?

A: Yes, my Mother. I'm sorry I left you.

Mother: I understand and I forgive you.

Once again, it is highly unusual, but I felt Anne's guides had one more life to show Anne. When I am facilitating a past life, I, too, many times go to an altered state of consciousness and many times, I feel the client's higher self influencing my actions, as well, through my spirit guides guiding me to pursue another past life.

L: I now ask you, Anne, to float above the scene of the bridge and the river and your body. Float your soul's essence to a clear sky with billowy clouds and then gently float down to a meadow of swaying grasses.

A: I see a baby in a cradle. I'm the mother.

L: How old are you?

A: I am 35 years old.

L: Can you tell me how you are dressed?

A: I have a white gown dress on, and I have long dark hair.

A: My husband has abandoned us. I am with a tribe. I am Native American.

L: What is your name?

A: "Saca-ja-wa-ya." It means a certain kind of flower in our language. I now see myself in a tent. He didn't abandon us. My husband was banished from the tribe. He was sleeping with another woman. Now the tribe is looking at me as not complying with their community because I don't have a husband.

L: What is happening now?

A: They are pushing me on men. The Chief is mad at me. But I still love my husband, even if he is gone. The tribe gets tired of me. I take my baby and leave.

L: Do you recognize the soul essence of your baby as anyone you know in your current life?

A: The baby is my sister, Sarah, today. My Native American husband is Charlie. He is a member of the Post Traumatic Stress Depressed Veteran group I currently attend. And we don't get along at all.

A: Sacajawaya tries to find another tribe to take her in. She gets stopped by a white man while on her journey. I defend my baby from him. I couldn't understand what

he is saying to me! He rapes me and he kills the child!
Then when he tries to kill me, I take the weapon, which
is a long knife, and kill him with it. Then I kill myself. I
couldn't live without my baby.

L: Now, once again, Anne, pull your soul essence away
     from the scene and float above it. Is there anyone you
     would like to say goodbye to?

A: My baby. I tried my best.

Baby: There is nothing else you could have done. You are a
       very strong person to have accomplished what you did.

L: Next, I would now like you to bring through your spirit
     guides on the count of three so that we may understand
     more fully these lives we have just experienced.

A: My master guide is showing me an expression of him
     which is protection. He is my connection to the fourth
     dimension.

L: What is that connection?

A: I have the ability to connect to the other side.

L: Any other guides coming through?

A: Lucas, and he is wearing a white hooded cape. He's
     very tall. He appears darker in the front of his being. He
     has two dark wings, also. He is keeping his head down.
     Now, he is giving me a headache. (Reminding her that
     is where her headaches are coming from.) Next, I see
     Jonah. He's very loving and lighthearted. Lucas says,
     "Pay attention to what we are saying to you. We will tell

you of these souls you think are stalking you." I can't keep ignoring them because I sense them all around me. I know, in my higher consciousness, what is going on. Some are trapped souls and just need to go to the light. They need my help, my guides say. One has been trying to connect to me in my dreams (the Native American she sees in her nightmares).

A: Yes, I am to be like a ghost whisperer. I am to help them cross over. Lucas will help me. The darker, one, Darius, will also help me.

L: What else do your guides want you to know?

A: I just don't want to mess it up. They tell me just to work from the heart in crossing the souls over. My guides are also telling me that I must do a ceremony over the deaths of Stephan and the baby. Lucas is saying to do a Native American ceremony for Stephan's burial. To finally bury him to release my pain over not having a proper burial for him. Also, for the baby, have a ceremony, to release the loss of my baby.

What Anne's spirit guides are describing is spirit attachment. As Greg McHugh, CCHt, describes this phenomenon in his book, *The New Regression Therapy, Healing the wounds and trauma of this life and past lives with the presence and the light of the Divine:*

> "For most of us, the normal process or route upon physical death is for our non-physical bodies or spirits either to go quickly or slowly into the Heaven World and the White Light of God. When this happens, there is initially a lifting out of the body and often the leaving of physical sensations. For a while we may remain in the consciousness which

was held while in the body and then, either quickly or gradually, we may feel relief from the physical constraints and the emotional dross. Some of us do not go into the light at death, however. Some of us remain here close to the physical plane for a while or what seems like a long time and then, upon letting go of whatever state we had been attached to, we are taken up into the light. When someone leaves the body but remains here, they may haunt dimensions close to the earth plane."[3]

For Anne, her spirit guides are referring to the work she is to do by using her ability to reach the 4th dimension to help these souls go to the light.

After the regression session, Anne discussed the severe headaches she had had lately. She now feels the guides were causing them to get her to wake up to her calling to lead the souls into the light. This would release their attachment to her. Anne also recalled to me that in her present life, she has always been afraid of wooden bridges. She will not walk or drive over them.

In addition, her knee gives her problems. Also, in her solar plexus there seems to always to be a pain and inflammation. Her solar plexus is where she was stabbed by the planks on the broken bridge in her life as a robber in Germany in the 1700s. The solar plexus is also where she stabbed herself fatally as a Native American when she realized she could not live without her baby. Anne said her

---

[3]Greg, McHugh, CCHt, *The New Regression Therapy, Healing the wounds and trauma of this life and past lives with the Presence and the light of the Divine, A Manual for Practitioners and Healers* (Denver, Colorado: Greg McHugh, CCHt, 2010), 100.

knee hurt exactly where she saw that her knee was amputated in the past life in Spain. These pains should greatly lessen or disappear eventually as she processes these past life experiences.

Many times the emotions we experience during traumas in past lives will settle into our present body in the location where the pain of the trauma occurred. These pains may beexperienced in many future lives until the client can re-live the past life to ultimately release it forever.

Anne's PLR case exemplifies just how devastating attachments can be to our soul's path in the present life. Without releasing the tie of the attachment from our lives, we cannot fully bring our soul's mission to realization. The attachments draw our physical and emotional strength from us. It's as if we have a debilitating disease in our mind, body, and spirit which must be attended to and healed. PLR is the perfect vehicle along with ascended beings of light in the form of spirit guides to bring the healing light to help with the cure.

Chapter Four
Cases For Parallel Lives

We are now discovering that linear-based human lives are not the only way to experience being on planet earth. It is also possible to have parallel lives, or two lives happening simultaneously or overlapping. Under a hypnotherapeutic trance state, several clients have revealed detailed and full lives that either overlapped their present life or parallel it for many years.

Dick Sutphen, the noted author and teacher on past life works, currently teaches a CD course called Parallel-Life Transfer Session. He has documented several of his clients' regressions by following up the details and traveling to locations to check facts of parallel lives. He states from his book, *You Were Born Again To Be Together*,

> "You are more than one person now living on the earth."[4]

---

[4]Dick Sutphen, *You Were Born Again to be Together*, (Charlottesville, Virginia: Hampton Roads Publishing Co., Inc., 1976), 25.

Parallel lives is one topic discussed in the *"Seth Speaks"* series of books by Jane Roberts. In The 1976 book, *Psychic Politics*, Seth channeled through Jane:

> "You can live more than one life in one time. You are neurologically tuned in to one particular field of actuality that you recognize." Seth also says in the book, "If you could think of a multidimensional body existing at one time in different realities, and appearing differently within those realities, then you could get a glimpse of what is involved." And later, Seth says, "You live more than one life at a time. You do not experience your century simply from one separate vantage point, and the individuals alive in any given century have far deeper connections than you realize. You do not experience your space-time world, then, from one but from many viewpoints."[5]

In 1999, Walter Semkiw, MD, researched a case of split incarnation in his book, *Born Again, Reincarnation Cases Involving International Celebrities, India's Political Legends and Film Stars.* Her name is Penney Peirce. She is a professional intuitive, counselor, perceptual skills trainer and lecturer who works throughout the United States, Europe and Japan. She is the author of *Frequency, The Intuitive Way and A Guide to Living from Inner Wisdom.* Penny discovered she had had a split incarnation through a medium who

---

5 Jane Roberts, *Psychic Politics*, (New Jersey: Prentice-Hall Publishing, 1976), 76.

connects to the Akashic Records, a set of memory banks or a library of the planet's history, found in the spirit world. The case of Alice Cary and Charles Parkhurst as a split incarnation in previous lives of Penney Peirce was revealed to her in detail by the medium. Penney was told she had been Alice Cary, born in 1820 and died in 1871, and that Charles Parkhurst was born in 1842, at a time when Alice Cary was 22 years old. In reviewing this chronology, we observe that there is an overlap of 29 years between Parkhurst's birth in 1842 and Cary's death in 1871. In this period of 29 years, it appears that the same soul was animating two bodies. Penney Peirce was born 16 years after Parkhurst's death. Alice Cary and Charles Parkhurst were authors and wrote many books. Alice Cary wrote, among others: *Poems of Alice and Phoebe Cary, Clovernook, Recollections of Our Neighborhood in the West and Hagar: A Story for Today.* Charles Parkhurst had written many books, among them: *The Sunny Side of Christianity, A Little Lower Than the Angels, What Would the World be Without Religion.*

Penney sped to the library after being told all this information and was able to verify all of the dates and the many books. She found that she and Charles both had an interest in spirituality and provided service through the ministry. In researching Alice Cary, she found her to be a social activist, like Penney. Plus, they all resembled each other in looks from pictures Walter Semkiw was able to find. All three lived close to each other, as well, in Massachusetts. Penney concluded that the information was correct and that her soul had experienced parallel lives or split incarnations.[6]

---

6 Walter Semkiw, MD, *Born Again, Reincarnation Cases Involving International Celebrities, India's Political Legends and India's Political Legends and Film Stars,* (New Delhi, India: Ritana Books, Defense Colony Flyover Market, 2006),147-163

In 2011, one client of mine, William Harrelson, experienced a very detailed past life that was paralleling his own life for many years. William is a service manager for a new car dealership and is a very high-energy person. He is in his 50s, yet looks and acts like someone much younger. He is about 5'6" tall and very wiry and lean in build. Midway in his regressed trance, William's parallel life became clear.

W: It's nighttime. I am in a large room. There are finishes on the ceiling. It's a comfortable home.

L: Can you describe what you are wearing?

W: I have boots on, Levi's and a t-shirt with the sleeves cut off. (This dress alerted me that the scene he was experiencing was present day.)

L: Can you describe what you look like, as if you held an imaginary mirror up to your face?

W: My hair is light, cut short. I have a dark short beard. I have a handkerchief around my neck. I am in my 30s.

L: Do you know your name?

W: My name is Bert. I am alone in the house.

L: Do you know the year you are in?

W: It's 1963, I live with my parents.

L: Do you recognize the location?

W: It's Maine.

L: Please proceed to tell us what you do next.

W: I am going downstairs to eat. My mother is in the kitchen. It's dark, so it must be supper.

W: Dad is out doing chores. I am just visiting. I own my own house. It's ten miles up the road. I am an auto mechanic. I am married to Linda. My wife is a stay-at-home wife. And we have no children.

L: I ask William if we can move to the next most important scene in this past life on the count of three.

W: I see a boat. It's my boat. It's a ski boat. It's my friends and me. It's just the boys. We are in the water. I am driving the boat. I don't like to ski. Now, we are finished skiing. It's the end of the day. Home is 25 miles away. We stop to eat and then we all go home. Why am I being shown this scene? I am not sure..............

W: Next day I am with the horses. I am in a corral. There are twenty of them in the corral. I love horses. I pet them and talk to them. I am like a horse whisperer. I saddle up and ride one. I am riding in the range. It's quiet and the early part of the day. I come back and give the horse a workout. Then I have lunch.

L: Once again, I ask William to move further in his life as Bert. On the count of three we are there.

W: Now I see that I am a builder. I am now in my 50s. I have two children. I am building houses and teaching my son, Jim, to do the same. I have five or six guys working for me. They are all very busy. I am happy and I am very positive about my life.

L: I now ask William to move to the last day of his life as Bert in this "parallel life" he is experiencing.

W: It's the last day of my life. I am going to be cremated. I have one brother. My friends, my children, and my wife are all here to be with me. I am only 55 years old. Now I see that I am being cremated.

I now ask for William's soul to rise above the scene and float up to a higher realm. In this higher realm he can connect with his spirit guides to gain more insight into why he was shown this parallel life.

W: Mish appears (his master guide). He is 5'6" tall with dark, wavy hair. He is small, but powerful. Mish is strong with a good side and a bad side to his personality. He says that my mission in life is to be strong, not weak, and to be honest and hard-working.

L: I ask his master guide, Mish, "Is it possible to live two lives simultaneously?"

W: Yes. No problem, my guide says, to live two lives at the same time. It's to show people that it can be done.

In my regression work, I find that it takes the more advanced soul who is stronger and more resilient to take on the challenge of two parallel lives to accomplish faster soul growth and resolve karmic lessons.

What was the other life lesson for Bert about? Mish says that it was to show William how lucky he is. He is the stronger of the "soul splits." The other soul split is dying at a young age of 55 (we saw that Bert died in the year 2018 which, of course, is in the future and is still to happen) because he did not take care of himself and he was not as strong a human specimen as William is. Mish says that usually when there is a soul split, one is weaker than the other. The message for William is to live your life to the fullest. Mish says that William is happier, and with more people in his life to love him than Bert. He ends with saying that William is on the spiritual path that he came to follow.

It's very interesting that both men were mechanics when they were younger, but that only William continued with the work by going into management. He even had an advanced degree in management for his job. The master guide chose to show himself much like William. He was short, but very strong. We didn't see the whole life of Bert, but it appears that he had some health problems and died at a young age. Whereas William prided himself on eating healthy and living a healthy lifestyle. It's almost as if his higher soul could see what not do to by Bert's actions in his life in Maine, so that William would not repeat them.

The next case was a young woman by the name of Allie Holter. Allie didn't have any particular questions about past lives. She just wanted to see and experience a past life or lives. Allie easily went into trance and she saw a life as a man in France.

A: I am outside in a meadow.

L: What are you wearing?

A: I have on fine boots, pants, and a jacket. I have short dark hair.

L: Can you tell me how old you are?

A: I am a male in my 30s.

L: Do you get a sense of the country you are in?

A: There are forests, trees, and I am walking in the forest. I see deer. It is in Europe. It is in France. There are others here. We are being closed in. We are all strangers. We are hiding because it's war........

A: I don't live around there. I have no family. My parents were French Jews. I now go back out to the edge of the forest and walk along the edge to see if anyone is following us.

L: I ask Allie to move us to the next most important scene in this past life on the count of three.

A: I am inside. The place has wooden floors and windows. There are other people with me. I am now in my 60s. I am married and my wife is here with me. We have a table in the kitchen and chairs. It's a very simple home.

A: Now I am sad. I see that I am all alone. I am in the country by myself. I am very isolated. I don't see or talk to many other people. I am in good health. My name is Rene. I loved my wife and I am sad because she is gone. We had three children but they have all moved to bigger cities to live. I feel so alone. I sense that my wife is the soul essence of my mother, Sondra, in my present life. My wife has been gone a long time. I see myself getting up and walking around in the house. I am picking up an ax and chopping wood. I am a farmer and I grow vegetables. Now I see that I am back in the house and I am just sitting at the table thinking about the past.

L: I ask Allie to move to the last day of her life as Rene.

A: I am in a bed by myself. My chest is constricted. I had a heart attack. I am in my 70s.

L: Let your soul rise above your body now, and begin to float away. You will not feel any pain as you move on up into a higher vibrational realm where you will meet your spirit guides.

A: I feel a female, and she is giving me a lot of warmth. She tells me her name is Simone. She is strong and tall. She is a light being and she is leaning over me. She gives me protection and is always watching out for me. There is also a masculine presence to the left of Simone. I feel this masculine presence around me a lot.

L: Please ask Simone why you were shown this past life today.

A: The fact that Rene was alone for a great period of time in his later life. We want Allie to recognize that she is repeating his life by being so very alone again in her present life. Allie asks her guides if she will ever be settled. (She travels for work and goes to foreign countries for her work. She thinks nothing of doing this singular work, yet she is only in her 20s.) They tell me that I have closed myself off from others. Because of the many lonely years as Rene, I have felt comfortable being alone myself.

L: Allie wants to know of her life's path from her guides. She also has a life-long friend, Mica, that she wants you, her guides, to tell her about.

A: My guides say that I identify with Mica. He is Jewish (she is not.). He is so happy in this life. Simone says I should learn how to be like him. She says you do not have to be alone. We can help you learn how to open yourself up to others.

A: Why do I struggle so with Mica? He was not in this previous life as Rene..... Simone says because I am still resentful from the life as Rene. I was like a bitter old man. I felt abandoned. My kids even left me when they grew up as adults. And why am I so restless? Simone says that I am preventing myself from fully enjoying life because I always leave for the next assignment for work. Simone says that Rene was an orphan and that he craved being with people, but was stuck in the country and could not move because he had the farm and home. You as Allie are determined not to be stuck in one place, so you move around all the time.

A: My guides are telling me that within ten years Mica will still be in my life, and, by then, he will teach me how to be happy.

After Allie sat up and came out of trance, we discussed the timing of the past life. Rene died in the 1980s and Allie was born in 1979. So clearly there were a few years of simultaneous, parallel lives that have clearly affected how she has lived her life. The loneliness of Rene's life emotionally stayed with her in today's life as Allie. She must try hard to release this feeling of loneliness. Her mother was her wife in this past, parallel life, and wants nothing but her happiness in this present life. Her higher self probably knew that Allie needed to touch these feelings of loneliness from this parallel life in order to release it, and release the feelings for good.

Most recently, a client came to me feeling very depressed and negative. She hoped that by looking at past lives she could uncover the cause for her depressed feelings. Here is the parallel life as it unfolded for Sharon Landry:

S: I am inside a big empty room. Next, I move out to an open meadow. It's sunny, and I see trees, plants and flowers.

L: Could you describe what you are wearing?

S: I have on tennis shoes, pants, and a tank top. I have dark, short hair.

L: What is your name?

S: My name is Karen. I am 17.

L: What is the year? Let me know the first number that comes to your mind.

S: The year is 1974. I am by myself. I am getting away from something. Mom is a stay-at-home mom.

L: And your father?

S: My Dad is not there. They are separated. I am getting away from Mom. I work in town. It's Kansas or Nebraska. I am sitting in the park and watching people. I do not have a boyfriend. I have a younger sister.

L: Let's move to the next most important scene in this past life of Karen's that we are currently viewing on the count of three.

S: I am living on my own. I am in my 20s. We are together. My boyfriend, Corey, and I are together.

L: Do you recognize the soul essence of Corey as anyone you know in your present life?

S: Yes, Corey is my friend, Todd, today. Corey is mean to me. He yells at me a lot. He leaves. I am a waitress. I stay to myself.

L: Let's move to the next most important scene on the count of three.

S: I am in my 40s. I am still a waitress. I am kind of shy, and I have never married. I don't want to get mixed up with another "Corey." The collie I have as Karen is my dog "Tike" who's with me now.

L: Let's move to a later scene in Karen's life on the count of three.

S: I am in my 60s and I am in an assisted living home. I have trouble getting around. I am sad and lonely. My mom and dad are gone. I never did get a relationship developed with my dad.

L: Let's now move to the last day of your life as Karen on the count of three.

S: I am ready to go. I am in a bed at the assisted living facility. I am 78 years old. (The year of her death would be 2035.)

L: As your soul now floats up above your body, allow it to float to a higher vibrational realm. This is now a wonderful time to call in your spirit guides to learn more about the past life you just experienced.

S: I feel warmth, wisdom, fatherly love, and a personality like old man winter. He would like to be called "Father." I also feel a Native American guide around me. I see that he has his shirt off, buckskin pants and a feather in his hair. His name is Lonewolf. I see that a third guide is showing himself as a bird.

S: My guides are telling me that this life of Karen's is a parallel life. The life of Karen is the life I, too, am going to experience if I don't make changes. My spirit guides are saying that I have to find a way of giving, but also take care of myself. Being somewhat selfish will make me happier in my life. Being good to myself is uplifting for me, my guides say.

S: My spirit guides say that all males aren't horrible people. Corey caused me to dislike men. The things I am doing now are positive and the world won't come to an end when my child leaves to go away to school. (Sharon has been terribly worried about being alone when her son goes off to college.) Father and Lonewolf say that the parallel life of Karen is causing me the sadness and depression I am experiencing. They say to just keep being true to myself and to keep doing what I am doing and things will be getting better and happier for me.

Sharon's parallel life was going on almost simultaneously. Karen was born about 16 years before Sharon was born. But you can understand how Karen's alone life has affected the way Sandra responds to all events in her life. She has a feeling of hopelessness about her life. A mother would normally be feeling some loss at her son going away to college. However,

Sharon was terribly depressed and wanted to move to be closer to him at school.

Sharon found very little faith in finding happiness in a male partner in her future. Though she was still a healthy person and young enough to have a whole life still ahead of her, Sharon did not believe a caring relationship was possible for her. These feelings were coming through her soul that was sharing the life as Karen, who was very sad and alone. Karen's aloneness was of her own choosing. Sharon's spirit guides were telling her this did not need to be her fate also. She must keep living for her own happiness in order to break out of the pull of this parallel life she was dealing with from Karen's life, which is still existing. Sharon decided at the end of her session not to move to Arizona, but to stay here when her son went off to college.

One of my most recent clients, Robin Risner, came to me for a past life regression in April of 2012 to investigate why she had so much pent-up anger inside of her. She also had trust issues in relationships. She told me that she had a dad who was not close to her and a step-dad who was critical of her while she was growing up.

Robin began the scene lying out on the ground, looking up at large trees.

R: I see lots of oak and sycamore trees.

L: Can you tell me what you are wearing?

R: I am barefoot, and I have on shorts and a t-shirt. My hair is long and dark.

L: How old are you?

R: I am in my 40s. My name is Destiny. I am just hanging
      out by myself. It's very peaceful here.

L: Are you married?

R: No. I am single. I do have a child. It is far away.

L: What country are you in?

R: It's far away. It's a different continent, the UK....... Now
      I am hiking and there is a big lake in front of me. (Robin
      decided later that it was the ocean.) I am by the beach.
      There are people around me, but I do not know them.
      I am picking up stones. It's a rocky beach and I am
      looking for stones. I am looking at the lighthouse at
      the end of the beach, next to the water. It's a lighthouse
      way, way out.

L: I ask Robin to move to the next most important scene in
      Destiny's life on the count of three.

R: The lighthouse is really big. It is at the coastline where
      it juts out. I am waiting for something. There is a big
      winding staircase inside of the lighthouse. I can see the
      wooden pillars on the inside of the lighthouse. I played
      there when I was young. I like to be where it is high. It
      reminds me of the church with the ringing church bells.
      I like to hear the bells and I like to be up high in the
      church where the bells are.

L: Tell me about your child.

R: He is a little boy. About 4-6 years old. His name is Max.
      He is blonde. (I recognize him as someone I knew in my
      life today for a short time. His name is John.)

L: Where is his father?

R: He is gone. He is close by, but not there in the same town. He comes and goes. But that doesn't mean in a bad way. He likes to travel. He is gypsy-like. The boy knows his father. I help out the elderly while I am waiting on Max's father to come home. We are very lower middle class. I see that we have very few material possessions. We are very rural. It's the early 1900s. I am helping the neighbors. I know everyone. People tell me stuff. I take my son with me everywhere. Max is very outgoing. No one is a stranger to him. My husband rarely comes to see us. I see that I make bread for a living. My mom is my mother in my present life, and my dad I recognize as my step-dad, Brad, in my current life. But they live really far away. I really like my life. I like to get away on long walks. I like to sit by the water. I know that my husband is coming back soon. I care about him. He just shows up. His name is Roy. He really is a free spirit. He cares for us, though, but he is very into what he does. He works with boats. He is very strong.

L: Is he a ship's captain?

R: Sometimes he takes on that role, but mainly he is part of the crew on ships.

L: Let's move to the next most important scene in Destiny's life on the count of three.

R: I am by the water. I am in my 60s. My son is in college, away. My husband, the ship's mate, still travels, but not as much. He sees me more often now. We are at a really sandy beach. It is Spain. I am happy. Roy likes to be on the water. I like to be by the water. I am very proud of

Max. He is very successful in school and he travels, too. I am enjoying myself. I like my independence. It's the 1960s.

L: I ask Robin to move to the last day of her life as Destiny on the count of three.

R: It's really cloudy and rainy. I am in northern England. I am at the cliffs next to the ocean. My son is here and his family is with him. He has two children. His wife I recognize as the soul essence of my friend Sharon in my life today. Max feels like a twin soul to me. He feels very much a part of me as my soul is ready to leave. I feel very tired. And it's time to go.

L: Allow your soul self to slowly float up above the scene and as it ascends upwards into a higher vibrational state, you are moving into a higher spiritual realm. (I ask that Destiny say goodbye to her loved ones to put closure to her life as Destiny. Then I ask her to ask that her spirit guides come through and help us with the life she just experienced. She realizes that her life as Destiny overlapped for many years her life as Robin.)

R: I am feeling a male guide. His name is John. He is calm and bringing many brilliant colors with him. Red, Orange, Purple, Blue. He is showing me a star shape but with rounded edges with all these colors. He moves very fast. I see my Grandma Dotty. I see my dog. I see my old friend Alexis.

L: Will your spirit guides speak to you of your parallel life as Destiny?

R: I have to believe in myself. It's okay. Just believe it's all going to be all right. Stop always thinking: "I should" be doing something else. Things are happening the way they are supposed to. Stop being so stubborn, they tell me. John says that I have to work on my trust for others. I talk myself down from doom and gloom. I can't expect everything to be perfect. Destiny had her life just like she wanted it. John says I have to have faith.

R: My Grandma Dotty says remember that Grandpa and I never slept together and we loved each other. John says that there is a man who will appreciate the different woman that you are. Yes, Max is your twin soul.

R: What about Roy? Have I met Roy in this present life? John says I haven't met the man that I will be with in the future, but he's out there. I feel it's the soul essence of Roy in Destiny's life.

This was a very complex life. Robin was feeling unfulfilled by the shortcomings in her present life. She compared her present life to the independent, unique life that her parallel life as Destiny was experiencing and felt hers didn't equal it. Robin was born about ten years before Destiny passed on. But the freedom-loving Destiny has certainly lingered with her in her present life. Hopefully, Robin will be more positive about her future. Her master guide has assured her she will meet the freedom-loving soul essence of Roy in this lifetime again.

This chapter really shows how parallel lives affect us for the good, and the not so good, in our present lives. Many times one soul life is weaker than the other with similar personality traits. Michael Newton, PhD, in his book, *Life Between Lives, Hypnotherapy for Spiritual Regression* (2004), states:

> Dim light (not to be confused with younger
> souls) is particularly evident with souls who

have chosen to live parallel lives in two bodies
in the same timeline. This practice, designed
to accelerate learning, is not encouraged by
guides for the average soul because it causes
such an energy drain.[7]

The goal is always to grow from all the relationships
we have, no matter how many parallel lives we are living in
to experience them.

---

[7] Michael Newton, PhD, *Life Between Lives, Hypnotherapy for Spiritual Regression,* (Woodbury, Minnesota: Llewellyn Worldwide, Ltd., 2009), 135.

CHAPTER FIVE
RELEASING PHYSICAL WOUNDS TO BRING JOY BACK TO THE SOUL SELF

The time will come
when, with elation
you will greet yourself arriving
at your own door, in your own mirror
and each will smile at the other's welcome,

and say, sit here. Eat.
You will love again the stranger who was your self.
Give wine. Give bread. Give back your heart
to itself, to the stranger who has loved you

all your life, whom you ignored
for another, who knows you by heart.
Take down the love letters from the bookshelf,

the photographs, the desperate notes,
peel your own image from the mirror.
Sit. Feast on your life.
>   *by Derek Walcott*
>   *Derek Walcott Collected Poems*
>   *1948-1984*

Many clients come to a regression therapist after all else fails to answer their needs. They are unhappy in their lives, suffering from unexplained physical ailments, and usually depressed. The unseen energies are their last hope for an answer and a solution to their trauma.

In April of 2012, a client, Donna Penny, came to me requesting a past life regression to determine whether her past was at the root of her complete lack of motivation in living her life. She felt she sabotaged herself and did not understand why she kept repeating self-defeating actions over and over in her life. Donna's spirit guides take her to the first most important scene in a significant past life as they show her a beautiful landscape with a sunny sky up above.

L: Describe for me how are you dressed.

D: I am dressed in boots, with work pants on and a jacket
.

L: Describe what you look like.

D: I am a male in my 20s and I have short black hair.

L: Please tell me what you see around you.

D: I see raised buildings with stairs from the ground leading up to the entrance ways. I am in a town, a village, and I feel other people are there. It is in the 1300s. The next thing I see is that in I am in a meadow and I am enjoying the day.

D: My name is Sam.

L: Where is your family?

D: They are not too far away. I am single. I left the family. I am young and I am enjoying looking at the mountains and hearing the birds.

L: Let's move to the next most important scene in your life as Sam.

D: It's dark and it's nighttime. There is a crowd by the buildings. It's a gathering of some kind. I am standing far away and cannot see what is going on. I am trying to go forward. There are angry people in the crowd. I am upset by the scene. I can't seem to see the crowd of people. I don't like crowds.

L: I was obvious that the essence of Sam did not want to get closer, but to see what was troubling Donna's higher self, she must see the scene. Would you please ask Sam to get closer to the angry crowd?

D: I am asking Sam to get closer. Someone is on the ground. It's a woman on the ground. She has been injured. She's crying. She's yelling at the angry crowds. They are hitting her with sticks and stones. I am that woman! I see gray mist. I think they killed me! I am angry with everyone because I was innocent of any crime. Strange, but Sam and I did not know each other in this life. He was just an observer to this angry scene.

L: At this point, Donna starts crying and continues to cry for the rest of the regression. She is releasing anger and pain that her emotional body has held onto for over 700 years.

L: I ask Donna to bring in her spirit guides on the count of three.

D: Auriel, her master guide, comes through first. And then Lion, who tells her he loves her, comes through next.

L: I ask Donna to ask her guides why she was shown this
      past life.

D: It seemed like I had done something sexual that was
      against our laws, but that is not correct. My guides say
      that they perceived me as odd, or not normal, like being
      strange (maybe I was homosexual) and they killed me
      for it. I was just being me. I was just being who I was
      and they did not like that. I didn't fit the role. It doesn't
      matter about the community, Auriel says. Auriel says
      that because of my anger and the betrayal I experienced,
      I don't trust men in general today. Auriel says I need to
      let this anger go……

D: Lion is here just for my emotional support. Why do
      I have such lack of motivation? I am afraid to be me.
      Because I was punished so severely for being different.
      I am afraid of being seen in the world in my present life,
      because I am still different. Auriel says looking at this
      past life will now help my motivation and will allow
      myself to be happy with being "me."

After the session, Donna was very tired and somewhat
shaken. I felt it was too much at that session to discuss what
she had just experienced. I hoped that in time, the regression
she saw would help her heal her emotions and release the
anger of that life. Her soul felt that she had been so unjustly
persecuted and killed for no other reason than being herself,
that the trauma was very deep in her soul.

I was able to connect with Donna several months later
and received an update from her. She mentioned that the
"Sam" character had been a personality that she had assumed
in other past life explorations. She said he either comes
through because she has a hard time examining her own
experiences or he is just armor against a stranger sharing

her explorations. What was new was that she had never named him before. The character now had a name, Sam. Donna said that my instructions at the end of the regression were helpful, but she had not released all the rage and hatred from that past life. The lion, as one of her spirit guides, had come to her to sooth her. Donna said he allowed her to bury her face in his huge mane. However, when Auriel came to her, she had not let him help her, and instead had pushed him away. Donna said that there was something more that needed to be released from the regression, but the span of time was just too brief to allow for it. She still carried the pain, she said. She felt it would take more than one session to allow her to fully release the hatred and anger.

Donna did, however, say that the chief benefit of the regression was that she can now recognize the block when it comes up in her present life. Instead of freezing or running away and crying, she can now understand the emotions and breathe through the experiences that bring these feelings on. Donna felt that just finding the root of something so deep is essential in eventually being able to pull it out.

Laura Donovan came to see me for a much different physical trauma that she KNEW came from a past life. She herself was a healer, having trained in Reiki and other healing arts. Laura had been born with a shorter arm on her right side that had no forearm. Her elbow had the extension of bone that had her hand attached to it. Laura told me she also had a very unusual birthmark on the back of her leg. She had always managed to do anything she wanted with her disabled arm and had had loving grandparents who had raised her. Her mother and father had a large family, and they felt that the grandparents would be able to spend more time with Laura than they. The questions she had for her past life regression concerned these two subjects. She wanted to look at her arm deformity and the family dynamics using past life regression therapy.

Laura: I am outside walking down rocks. It's a rocky slope. I see little flowers. I am in the country.

Lee: How are you dressed?

Laura: I have on sandals, I am short, blonde, and I have on a dress with a jacket over it.

Lee: What is your name and what is the date?

Laura: I am in my 20s. My name is Alice. It is the 1700s and I am walking into town. I see stone buildings. I have a bucket of clothes under my arm. I am going to the stream. I am happy. My parents are alive.

Lee: Let's move to the next most important scene in Alice's life on the count of three.

Laura: I am older. I am in my 30s and I am married. We don't seem happy together. I have four children. I see that three of them are my children today, Drew, John and Fred. I don't know the fourth child in my present life. We are struggling. My husband is not around all the time. He is in shipping. He works on ships and he is gone a lot. I wash clothes for other people to bring in money for the family. We don't live in town, but the outskirts of town. My shoulder is hurting from carrying all the clothes.

Lee: Let's move now to the next most important scene in your life as Alice on the count of three.

Laura: I am in my late 40s or early 50s. There is a son and a daughter with me. They are adults. They help me with the clothes by carrying them for me. I can't carry much anymore. The son is my son Fred in my present life, and the daughter is my grandchild, Cindy, in my present life. My husband died at sea. The other two children have grown up and moved away from our little village. It is somewhere in Holland. We are Dutch.

Lee: Laura had an uneventful death at age 60 and she said she was ready to go. She was ready to leave this very hard physical life. As she floated above her body and rose away from that previous life, I asked Laura to bring through her spirit guides to give us more information about this past life as Alice in Holland.

Laura: My master guide is dressed like a jester. He is sitting on my legs. He is very protective of me. I ought to know him by now, he says. He's funny. He is tall, 7-8 feet. He is very tall. He has a box-like hat, tight pants and he is dressed very colorfully. He says that he can blend in anywhere as well. He dresses in camouflage colors very quickly. His name is George the Jester. He is still sitting on my legs.

Lee: Please ask George about the past life you just experienced.

Laura: I had to do so much of the work in this past life with the husband gone all the time. I had parents, but they didn't help me. They didn't like who I married. Now, it's the opposite in this life. My parents and grandparents adored me and treated me very well. (Laura is in her late 60s at the present.) The arm is teaching lessons to souls. Not teaching my siblings, but my mother and her mother (my grandmother) are learning from my deformity. They were the parents in the Amsterdam life. They left Alice.....

Laura: The birthmark is in the shape of an anchor. It is tied to this life of being around shipping and raising my kids around the water.

Laura: I am still teaching today. My granddaughter had twin boys and one has cystic fibrosis. She goes through a lot with him. He teaches a lot to other people about what's important. My granddaughter is learning about empathy for disabilities. (She was one of Alice's daughters in the Amsterdam life.) Cindy was raised by Laura and has empathy for all disabilities. George is saying it is okay to help her work with the school system to include kids with disabilities.

Laura was able to give herself love for the life she has taken on in her present life. Her arm was the same arm (right) she had used to carry clothes all those years in the life in Amsterdam. It was karmic contract with her family to resolve the past relationship with parents and grandmother in the present life from the one we saw in the 1700s. Laura knew this in her heart. I was just helping her to confirm what her heart already knew.

Physical trauma from a past life experience can cause the soul self to attach to events that were around the physical trauma. This next case is a good example of this. I met Charlotte Thomas in Sarasota, Florida, in May of 2011. She requested we look at old patterns she had in her life. "I am too money-oriented. I judge people by their money. I have no affection for them, just the money attachment is important for me. Is it to buy love?"

The first scene Charlotte sees in her regressive trance state is a forest.

C: It is very green here. I am in an oak forest. I am anxious. I am walking in the forest. I am young and I have long blond hair. There is a big tiger with a big mouth. I am trying to go past him. It is a test you have to pass to walk in the forest. The bright sun is coming in. The sun is shining in my face. I am out of the forest...... Now I see a small town. It is in a desert. There are people around. My face feels dry and wrinkled. I am wearing long clothes that are worn for the time. Scarves over my head and long skirt. It is A.D. around Jesus's birth. It is in Palestine. I am a young lady. There is a deep well. It is very hard to go to the well. It's where they take the water out. It's a well of gold now. I see myself taking a bucket of water out. The gold is solid gold. There is water under the gold. It makes me sad. The pain my husband has caused others to retrieve the gold is a tragedy.

L: Let's move to the next most important scene in this past life you are currently experiencing.

C: I am sitting in a small tent. There is food in my hand and I am in a yoga position. There is no laughter. It is serene. No family around. I have two small children. They are a boy and a girl. They are 8 and 12 years old. Their names are Eric and Natasha. My name is Anna. He is around. My husband is horrible. He is the king. Hercules is his first name. He has black hair and a harsh face. He has black eyes. He has huge power. He has a big scar on his face. He is very manipulating. He treats us very badly. I feel powerless. I am controlled. I am sad. The gold is his. I have no friends. There are just servants around us. The children are loving and they want to protect me..... I cannot leave. I cannot risk what would happen. I will be burned if I leave. I am like his toy, his prey. I do love him, however. There is no way out. His head is always above me. He's abusive. He beats me on my face and my right side. He rapes me. He yells at me. He spoils me at the same time. He hits me. I show my face because I am queen. I don't want to be.

L: I ask Charlotte to move to the next most important scene in her life as Anna on the count of three. What do you see now? Who is with you now?

C: I cannot move! He hit me and killed me! I am full of blood and I am lying on the floor.

L: I ask Charlotte to rise above the scene and pull away from her body. Please tell me who you see in the scene now.

C: A few days later I see myself still lying there on the floor and my unborn baby is still in my body. The baby dies, also. I see that the king is my ex-husband, Carl, today in my present life. He cheated and lied to me in my present life. He is repeating this past life in his present life. Natasha is my daughter in my present life, Anuska. I do not recognize the boy as anyone in my present life.

L: I now ask Charlotte to say goodbye to this life. The king can no longer control you. I now want you to bring through your spirit guides to help us understand why they showed you this past life as Anna.

C: I hear that my master guide's name is Tim. He has black hair and is wearing a suit. He is very formal. He is wise and funny. A group of the rest of my guides stands behind him.

L: Ask Tim how this past life helps you understand your issue with money.

C: All my lives, I see that for many, many lives I have come back to work on this issue that was caused by this trauma to me from the king. In this life, I have almost released it. This past relationship with Hercules was all about learning to love myself. Until then, I will not be able to love others. I must learn to be me and like me. All the guides behind me are happy! They are saying hallelujah!

Charlotte also felt guilt about the gold. Her husband the king controlled the water because it was used to get to the gold. So the village, as well as Anna, was under his control. She was so diminished in her self-esteem by him that she has spent many lifetimes getting over the severe physical trauma he put her through in this past life in Palestine. Charlotte is now learning to move forward and love herself, her guides tell her. While it seems her ex-husband, Carl(the king, Hercules) still has emotional traits from this past life he has not resolved.

Aaron Anderson was referred to me during a regression clinic I was giving in Denver in October, 2011. What make this case so interesting were the many lives shown by Aaron's spirit guides. It was the first occasion I had had to facilitate four very important past lives that all had a common thread. Physical trauma was involved in all four of Aaron's lives, which clearly affected him in his present life.

He came to get insight into his injuries. Aaron was hurting himself often and not healing from his injuries. He had been to medical doctors and was finding very little relief. Aaron quickly went into a light trance and his first very important scene opened on a hillside with a stone path.

L: Can you tell me what you are wearing?

A: I have on sandals. I am a Roman soldier. I am in armor with a red shawl draped over the armor on one side. I have on a metal helmet. I am a 27-year-old man.

L: Can you tell me your name and what year it is?

A: My name is Vesuvius. It is 342 A.D. I am anxious. I see a flash of battle in front of me. I am in the middle of the battle. Now I am looking at the battle from above. I see myself raising my sword. I see that I got stabbed by a spear with a red tassel hanging from it. I see smoke around me. As I lie dying, I look up to see a clear blue sky. I did not want to be there. My life was not complete when I died. I was a single man. There was no time to live my life before I had to go off to the big battle. I did not want to be there!

L: As I am inquiring about the end of his life as a Roman soldier, Aaron quickly sees the following scene.

A: My foot is nailed to a cross. I am strapped in on this cross.

L: Can you tell me what you look like and what you are wearing?

A: I have on a green shirt and around me it's all dirt and it's dark and I am alone.

A: I feel there is someone to my left below me.

L: Can you tell me the year you are in?

A: It is right before the time of Jesus's death. The year is 63 A.D.(sic) I have been on this cross for 2 or 3 days. I feel dirty and I have on loose-fitting pants with a rope belt. My hands are tied up to the cross. I have dark hair. My name is Jonah.

L: Do you have any family?

A: The woman to the left has a hood on. She is my wife. Her name is Sarah.

L: Do you recognize her soul essence as anyone you know in your current life as Aaron?

A: Yes, she is my ex-girlfriend, Carrie........ I am 23 years old. I was caught stealing bread. I feel like I want to cry. This situation is so sad for my family. I was trying to feed my family. I have a boy, a son, ten years old. His name is Samuel.

L: Do you recognize his soul essence as anyone you know in your life today?

A: Yes, he is my best friend, Rob. I see myself taking the bread. It's a real gloomy time for us. There is a plague going around toward the time of my being on the cross. There was not a lot of food for us. I was hiding with the bread when they caught me. This is a bad time for us all.

L: As Jonah dies on the cross, I ask him to gently pull away
      from his body and float up above the scene. I could feel
      from his guides that he was ready to drop into another
      past life. I ask him to visualize a meadow and slowly
      drop down into this meadow and tell what he saw in
      the scene before him.

A: I am a pope. I have on a regal red robe with black trim.
      I have a gold scepter with me. I am standing in a castle.
      I am a Catholic Archbishop! My name is Archbishop
      Michael. It is Rome, Italy. It is the 1200s. I am
      standing and speaking in front of thousands. They like
      me. I am their religious leader! I can see the crowds
      cheering. I am loved. But now I see that I am betrayed.
      I was emotionally stabbed in the back. I was actually
      poisoned. I was 43 years old when I died. I don't get
      the feeling that I knew what was happening to me. The
      betrayal was done by my assistant. There were 7-8 in
      the group below me that were the religious leadership.
      They sent my assistant to kill me. I see the group all
      wearing white with red trim.

L: Do you recognize any of the members as anyone you
      know in your life today as Aaron?

A: My assistant is a roommate of mine in college, today.
      Joseph, in the leadership group, was the leader who had
      me killed. I don't recognize him. I see him in white
      and he has black curly hair. Once more I ask Aaron to
      pull away from his body and float above the scene. As
      he is instructed to float down to a beautiful meadow, I
      get the sense from his guides that there is more to see.
      As he lands in the meadow, I ask Aaron what he sees
      before him.

A: It's World War II and it's in the 1940s. I am French. I'm a foot soldier.

L: Can you describe what you look like?

A: I have on a helmet, I am carrying a gun. I see barbed wire. I am in the middle of battle. I have been cut on the same arm that I am having so much trouble with concerning my tendon in my life today. (Aaron has had surgery to repair a tendon in his arm that will not heal properly.)

A: My name is Frank and I am 17 or 18 years old.

L: On the count of three, let's move to the next most important scene in this past life of Frank's.

A: I have been stuck with a bayonet. Now I see that it is years later. Ten years later. Part of me is still there on the battlefield. Some of my soul energy was left there. My guides are showing me that I am standing up and reaching out and bringing that part of me to the present in my life today.

L: As Aaron's soul floated away from the scene, he experienced receiving, in this life, a lost part of himself. I then asked for him to bring in his spirit guides for further information about these past lives.

A: I see an image of three or four beings. They are appearing in clothes Jesus would wear. I see them in white robes. My master guide comes forward and his name is John. Next, I see a Native American guide. He has paint on his face, and a bandana tied like an Apache's. He has on leather clothing with blue and white paint on his face.

He has dark skin. His name is Little Big Foot and he is a warrior.....Finally, I see a man in a top hat and tuxedo. It's the dress of the early 1900s. I see a carriage he is showing me. He is French. His name is Francois.

A: John says I am on the right track for my health, but I need more. I need energy healing now. I have done all the medical procedures to correct much of my pain, but the energy healing is still needed.

L: I had previously asked Aaron what procedures he was doing. He said that acupuncture and naturopathic remedies were being tried, but with only limited success.

A: My guide John says that there is a physical system problem. Endocrinology will help. I will be on the right track if I look into my endocrinology system.

Together, we drew conclusions from the series of past lives Aaron had been shown.

1.   Aaron had held onto all these injuries for so many years and so many lifetimes.
2.   He kept going back to very physical, violent lives.
3.   When Aaron experienced a past life during World War II in France, his higher self splintered from the heartache of being unable to be of greater help.
4.   He wanted to fulfill his goal of helping others, whether it was in battle or with his family.
5.   He was giving up his spirit to help others, once again.
6.   Fortunately, his spirit guides helped him pull pieces of his spirit back into the present physical body of Aaron to make his soul complete again.

Now he can start anew. Aaron had not loved himself enough in any of the past lives we visited. And he told me later that he felt he deserved the betrayal in his life as archbishop. Aaron said that his heart as an archbishop was selfish and egotistical.

The running theme in this chapter has been that when we do not love ourselves enough, we suffer from physical misfortunes by others. These physical traumas stay with us in the form of physical, mental, and emotional scars. These cases give evidence that we carry these scars forward to our present lives. There is only one answer for all of us to remember. Love begins with love for ourselves, before we can give love to others.

As Pema Chodron states in her book, When Things Fall Apart (1997):

> Everything that occurs is not only usable and workable but is actually the path itself. We can use everything that happens to us as the means for waking up. We can use everything that occurs—whether it's our conflicting emotions and thoughts or our seemingly outer situation—to show us where we are asleep and how we can wake up completely, utterly, without reservations.[8]

---

[8]Pema Chodron, *When Things Fall Apart*, (Massachusetts: Shambala Publishing, Inc., 1997),123.

CHAPTER SIX
FEELING STUCK IN LIFE

> Your pain
> is the breaking
> of the shell
> that encloses
> your understanding
>   *Kahlil Gibran*
>   *The Prophet*

When I met Vanessa Collins, in October 2011, I saw a tightly composed woman of about 50 years of age. She had four grown children, she told me, but did not elaborate in our first meeting. What Vanessa wanted from a past life regression session was freedom from being "stuck in her life." She said she had taken massage training, but could not ignite within herself any motivation to use her training. She felt she had other healing abilities, but could not overcome this feeling of "not being able to move forward in my life." Vanessa told me that she wanted to investigate past lives. She felt that here she would find her answers to her "stuckness" from past lives that were still affecting her life today.

Vanessa went into trance easily, though her body remained very stiff and tight. She immediately saw a very short scene of a life in which she had worked with magic to help her village in the year 1000 A.D. in Roman days. She wore a white gown and sandals and was in her 30s. Her name was Angelica. The Roman soldiers came to their village and almost killed her for the magic she practiced. They did put her in prison, but she was spared death because she was a woman.

Almost immediately, Vanessa was shown another life. This was also one quick overview, but the emotions she felt were significant. She was a peasant about 20 in the 1600s in England. The scene moves on and she sees herself married in her 30s and she has four children, two boys and two girls (four children as in her present life). She saw that her husband was the soul essence of her brother, Dick, today. Her husband did blacksmithing. All of a sudden she sees raiders to her community. They begin burning the buildings and killing everyone. The raiders wanted the land they had. Vanessa sees that they kill her entire family including herself by burning the house they are in. All die in the flames.

I knew by the traumatic emotional nature of these two lives, Vanessa's spirit guides wanted her to understand something very important. As we bring her guides through after these two lives had ended, her spirit guide, Aryon, came through dressed in a long robe with long blonde hair. Another guide was a Native American, named White Buffalo. He had on leather pants, a shirt, and a feather in his long black hair. He told her he helps her with her healing work today. A crow showed up and he stated that he works with magic. He wanted to be called Blackie.

Aryon told Vanessa that she has carried this anger from these two experiences for many, many reincarnations. But not only does she carry anger, but rage for people in general. Aryon said she needed to start trusting and forgiving others. He went on to say that she had experienced many lives such as this and the only way to "unstick" herself was to view more past lives to release the anger and rage. Aryon said she could release major blocks for herself in this way.

Our next session was not so fast paced. Vanessa's higher self and her spirit guides wanted to immerse her more in this past life to truly understand her relationship to the people she connected with in this past life in Germany.

V: I see that I am outside. There are big, tall buildings around me.

L: Please describe to me what you are wearing and what you look like.

V: I have on flats, with white nylon tights. I have a dress on over the tights. I have medium brown hair that is curly. I am in my mid-20s.

L: What is your name?

V: My name is Morgan. I am going to a party. It's daylight but about dusk. I walk a long way to meet friends. I do not have just one boyfriend. I like to party. I meet my friends and we go to dance. I meet a man and end up going to his place. His name is Jerry and we have sex. I fall asleep. I get up early the next day and leave before he wakes up. I am very promiscuous.

L: Do you have a job?

V: Yes, I am a secretary. My friends are from work. We work and then we party afterward.

L: Let's now move to the next most important scene in your life as Morgan on the count of three.

V: I am on a train. I am 40 years of age. I am trying to run away from someone I know. I have fear about this relationship. It was just an acquaintance, but he wants to do me harm. I know things. He told me things that are confidential. I see that I stop at a town. I am walking in the town. He is here! His name is Bernard. He chases me and catches me. Bernard has several people with him, soldiers in uniforms. They are Nazi German soldiers. They get me in an alley. These soldiers have guns. I know too much. The four soldiers shoot and kill me.

I ask Vanessa to slowly leave her body as Morgan. Let her soul self rise above the scene. And as she feels no pain or discomfort, I ask Vanessa to allow her soul self to expand and to feel strong again. Next, I ask her to please invite her spirit guides once again to come through and help us understand this past life as Morgan that she just experienced.

V: White Buffalo comes through. This is my Native American spirit guide. The whole Nazi German life was about fear. He is saying I knew there was more to it than people thought. There were many evil people involved in that war besides the Nazis. I just wanted to have fun and party, but I should have done more and been more responsible with the information I had about the evil that was going on around me. White Buffalo is telling me that I am too dependent in my current life. I am afraid to strike out on my own because of this life in Germany.

L: Can you ask White Buffalo what you should be doing for your life's path?

V: I am to use my healing abilities. He says he is helping to release the fear from this past life so that I can become "unstuck." Both White Buffalo and Aryon tell me that if

I would have more faith in myself in this life, they could help me more. But that I must ask for their help. They are always with me, my guides say.

The after session from this past life revealed more much for Vanessa. She said the four soldiers who shot her in the Nazi Germany life are the same souls that are her four children today. We discussed her children for the first time. All four suffered from drug and alcohol abuse. I would suggest that the guilt over having to kill one of our loved ones from our own soul group is a heavy burden for any soul to conquer. We didn't identify the four children she raised in the previous past life as a peasant wife in England, but I would guess that they were the souls of her four children today as well. I hope that after revisiting this most traumatic life, Vanessa will be able to release her anger and rage and be set free to live her life more fully today.

To date Vanessa has not been able to pursue any additional regressions to help her in her quest to overcome her anger issues. But the initial sessions have helped her greatly.

In May 2012 Susan Williamson (client from Chapter 2) and I started a new PLR session. She particularly wanted to know why she was so "stuck" in her life. Her career seemed to be successful, but her emotional life was on hold. Susan asked if we could delve into the past concerning partners once again and see if that held the key. She wanted to "unstick" her life and move forward.

As always, Susan goes into trance very easily and we move to the first important scene in her past life.

S: I see that I am outside among hills. There is a walkway on the grass. I feel determined. I am walking with a purpose and to find answers to some dilemma.

L: What are you wearing?

S: I have on leather sandals that lace up my legs. I have a
      breast plate on. I am wearing a helmet and a short skirt
      made out of leather. My hair is brown and long. I am in
      my 30s or early 40s. My name is Gandor.

L: What year is it and what country are you in?

S: It is 39 B.C. and we are in Greece.

L: Please tell me what you see next.

S: I am looking over the mountains. I am looking at the
      skyline. I am trying to determine where to bring the
      troops with me. I am by myself. I am scouting out the
      area. I feel troubled. I might be the leader of the army.
      I am feeling the weight of the world on my shoulders.
      We must make decisions before sunrise. Everyone is
      asleep. I walk back to camp. I walk through the men
      sleeping. Some are working on tools.

L: I ask Susan to move to the next most important scene in
      this past life in Greece on the count of three.

S: We are in a tent. I am talking to officials about our
      line of attack. There is a woman with us. She is very
      strong. She is not a queen, but she has been appointed
      to help and advise us. She is a gifted woman. We call
      her a mystic. I don't fear her. I respect her. Her name
      is Diabla.

L: Do you recognize her soul essence as anyone you know
      today in Susan's life?

S: No, I know her soul, but I do not recognize her as anyone in my life today.

L: Please, what do you see next in the tent?

S: We are talking about the east side of the hill. That is where the men can come in. Diabla steps up and tells us to come over the hillside. The other officials say we would be vulnerable if we do that. One man says we must do it this way. His name is Borraz. He says she doesn't know war.

L: Do you know the soul essence of Borraz?

S: Yes, I recognize him as my step-dad, Darryl.

L: What does the group decide to do?

S: Borraz pushes men and intimidates people. They are all agreeing with him. One of younger men is trying to answer with another alternative. He suggests we split the men up and some stay down below on foot in the valley and some go up over the east side of the hill and attack from the top of the hillside. His name is Demitri.

L: Do you recognize his soul essence as anyone you know today?

S: Yes, I recognize him as my niece, Lisa, today. The guys are giving him a hard time. I like him. I have taken him under my wing. I am the commander. I decide that we are going to keep the arrows (men with bows and arrows) at the top of the hillside. Then we will bring the spear men on horses into the valley between the hilltops.

S: Diabla says don't put so many men down in the valley. Put some to back the men with bows and arrows. I say, "That's enough" and we go to eat.

L: I ask Susan to move to the next most important scene in Gandor's life.

S: I am on the horse. It's late in the day. I am making sure everyone is ready. The opponents are from Persia. I see the opponent. They are coming towards us and haven't seen us yet. We are waiting and hoping they don't see us. I have my arrow men shoot into the valley. Then more men come out of the hills to start fighting. They were caught by surprise in the valley. The arrow men have stopped coming. Next the spear men are coming. The Persian army didn't have many weapons. They were not prepared. Behind us, suddenly horses are approaching. I am calling to the men to get out. The horsemen are coming! Horsemen are running over my men like stickmen. They are slaughtering my men. My key men are there. Yet, the horsemen are just all over us like ants. I am down in the valley trying to find my key men.

S: This group on horses is an ally to the Persian army. But they are a different group. I don't recognize them. I am remembering what Diabla said. There are too many men in the valley on foot. I can see Borraz. He is crazed and killing anyone he can. The younger man, Demitri, is dead. All my men are dead. My horsemen fled to the forest. I am standing in the middle of the battlefield. I don't know what to do. It's over. All are dead. Diabla said this would happen. I am looking at the bodies and seeing if anyone is alive. There is so much blood. I am now back at the tent. I am seeing who made it back.

Not very many survived. Diabla is crying. She knew this would happen. She's fond of me, but she is telling me that I will be executed for this. I will be captured and killed. She's very wise. I just stand there. It's over.

L: On the count of three, move to the next important scene in this battle.

S: I am in chains. I was captured. There are lots of people throwing things and jeering at me. The smells are nauseating. I have been beaten. They are taking me to kneel before their ruler. They are going to execute me. They are poor and dirty. My ego is in disbelief that they won.

L: Do you leave behind a family?

S: I have a wife and kids, but I also have women when I want. The battle was my life. The men were my family. I want to die. I am in front of the king. He asks about Diabla. They find her dead. She killed herself. I see her as an angel. She is a protector for me. They executed me. They beheaded me.

L: I ask Susan to rise above her dead body and let her soul self expand and feel its full strength.

S: I am apologizing to my men after I left my body. The men are angry at me. Some feel differently. They feel it was an honor to die. Even at that point, after we are all gone and only in spirit, some men are going to avenge what I have done. Meaning that they will come back in spirit to another life to fight another day. I feel it was war. I am not willing to take on their anger. Borraz was an instigator to war and was always pushing the men. A lot of the men in this army are the men in my life today.

L: Who do you recognize as men in your life today?

S: I know that my dad was in the army in Greece. I see my ex-husband as one of the men. Some I recognize as other soul members of my soul group but not in my current life. I see that Mike (Susan's boyfriend) is just another soldier in this war we just lost. I see my friend Rob was there.

L: Could you ask your spirit guides to come through now, and help us understand this very important past life?

S: I see that Trevor is here. He is my master guide. Also I see that Fred is here as well as Dawn. I also see that Diabla, the mystic, is here. She is also a guide for me. They say that I requested in this life to know what it is like to be on the other side of a man's feelings. What it feels like to have a man in charge and in control over me. I have a desire to see a man and experience his going through the pain and the struggles of living in this life. I get frustrated now as men make decisions. I see that the decisions they make have repercussions. The men in my life have always made decisions for themselves, not for me.

S: All of this experience I am going through with men has to do with this Grecian life as Gandor. The most angry man was Mike. He is angry with women. He doesn't see what he does with women. He cares about them though. But this life is all about control for him. He didn't want to die in this war in Greece. He was young and it hurt him to see so may die. That life started all this wanting to be in control for him. ....We are soulmates, but I am strong and that frustrates him. These men, now in my life, were in this battle, yet many of their feelings are still repressed in this present life.

S: They know deep down inside that I wasn't to blame, but they still want this control they lost by getting killed under my command. And I wanted to know and understand what it was like not to have the choices. My dad was over me and controlled me in my present life. As a child, I would ask for him to spend time with me, and he never would.

S: I don't want the ego to make the choices in this life, my guides tell me. On that hillside, I had all the choice. Mike is teaching me. He has a big ego. I see how it affects others. I see how my ego affected others in that war. In the battle, I didn't understand how my ego affected all my men. Now, I am feeling the effects of the men's ego in my life as Susan.

S: Diabla just chose that life to incarnate. She guides me more than she is a participant in a human life with me. She is a spirit guide for me in my present life. She tells me that I have been growing in my present life. I have been learning the lessons I came to learn. I can relax.

Susan's spirit guides went on to tell her that she was linked to Mike, but that he had important milestones he had to accomplish without her. But that soon they would reach a lightness between them. "This entire relationship with Mike is to learn and understand my ego. I still have to gain control of my ego. It's our armor. Our ego tells us we are going to be safe, but it is an illusion," Susan said.

Today, Susan is making great strides in overcoming her ego. Recently she and Mike had a conversation that felt different, she said. It was a balanced coming together of our thoughts. Neither he nor I tried to control the other. She felt they showed mutual respect for each other.

Both of these clients, Vanessa and Susan, were experiencing major blocks in their present lives and I believe they had reached walls that they could not penetrate. In using past life regression therapy, they were able to open those walls, explain what paths they had both chosen in their present lives, and realize that these past lives helped them choose their present soul paths.

We are all on a continuous journey to understand our human relationships with others. We have human lives in order to appreciate love and forgiveness for ourselves and for others. Many times we cause harm to ourselves and to others in our soul's growth on earth. Yet, as we learn, we evolve to a higher vibration of service to others, and we appreciate the love that these souls give us in our present lives.

CHAPTER SEVEN
CHANNELING OUR SPIRIT GUIDES, ASCENDED BEINGS, OR HIGHER SOUL SELF

> It is a time to stand in our truth, perhaps as we never have before, and to call upon all others to stand in theirs, so that together we can raise the consciousness of the group soul---bringing healing, bringing forgiveness, bringing illumination to the living of our world. We are the caretakers of Gaia, each with an assignment----each with a key.[9]

With very advanced souls, many times the guides will not show a past life. They feel the communication from them is more important, and that past lives would not benefit the soul as much.

In researching cases for this book, I found several important messages that were brought through for all of us to hear. Whether they be through ascended beings who channeled through the client at the end of their past lives, or their own spirit guides who spoke through the client, or even the client's own higher soul self bringing these messages, these conversations were different than a typical client's

---

[9] Patricia Cori, *The Starseed Dialogues, Soul Searching the Universe,* (Berkeley, California: North Atlantic Books, 2009). Preface Page xii.

past life session. While I facilitated a regression, the client changed the mannerisms in their face, and they spoke with a different pronunciation of words. The depth and pitch of their voice changed as well. It was clear to me that the client was channeling a highly advanced being that had words for us all to hear concerning our living on planet earth at this very crucial time in earth's history.

Suzy Emmett is a psychic medium who "sees dead people." Suzy is a loving hospice nurse who has a smile and a twinkle in her eye for you every time she meets you. In January of 2012, Suzy ask me to do a past life regression with her. Her questions were similar to most. She wanted to know what her spirit guides could tell her that would help her on her path in her present life. In Suzy's regression session, she went straight to her spirit guides for answers to her questions and they gave her messages for all of us to hear.

L: Please tell me what you are seeing or hearing, Suzy.

S: It's daytime and I am with Jesus. He is whispering in my ear, "It's all about love." Jesus is saying that humans are in turmoil. Humans are having such a time rising above to see what is. "It is just as easy as walking on water, or making bread. It is so easy to rise above" he speaks through Suzy.

S: I am holding his hand. He is wearing sandals, with a loosely woven sheath on and a rope belt. He says that I am a soul essence of John. Jesus says he saw the potential but he also saw their fear. He knew what he had come to do. He knew that he would be killed. But he did not know that it would be so painful.

S: I am very careful with my words. Words have energy. He has been with me since I was born. All will happen in a magnified way, now. He is showing me all the grids. It will be within five years. The earth is now shifting. It's like a rock rolling down a hill and then it stops. But we will get another chance. Not all will get another chance. Many are getting caught up in the density. They are in the same field, but another dimension.

S: This is much of my sadness. People who are not believing me now. They believe the more traditional views of living. They believe lessons are less spiritual when they must go through a traditional teacher to learn these lessons.

S: Jesus says life is a paradox. We must feel all emotions. We choose a soul path to have emotions. In the last 50-75 years, we have become a culture of blame. In this year of 2012 there will be many diseases. In the first part of 2012 there will be natural disasters. It is to get everyone's attention. But some are still jumping onto fear. It's all about dimensions. We have "numbed out."........

S: Every healer is trying to listen with all their senses. It's an energy. It's a vibration. If they can't hold it for themselves, they can't hold it for another.

L: Can Jesus tell us about ascension?

S: Jesus tells me "Souls ascend and come back. At night, while we humans sleep, our souls get training to come back more enlightened. We fear our own strength, however. We are here to teach parents and children to love ourselves. People are becoming aware, but still there are many in darkness, and they are being pulled toward the darkness. As if in the Roman times, we need to learn how to exist in the light. Each pattern for each soul is different."

L: Are the dark forces being pushed out?

S: Jesus says that the next 18 months will be hard. This is like a training period. We have to see the bigger picture. Jesus says I have had many lives in the fairy world. In my younger life, the only way I could see them was to be upside down. I would walk on my hands when I was small. There was a large elf with me. That is how close the other dimension is where the fairies dwell..... When I see anger, it hurts my back (Suzy has severe back pain). I help many with their emotions. I help many as they cross over (in her role as hospice nurse). We all chose our life paths. But we simply can't remember that we chose the paths.......... As people learn now about their paths, we all should be having more love, but instead we have hate and anger. We don't allow the gift of love and time into our lives. We must learn to love ourselves......

S: It's possible to walk on water to feed the hungry. We are healing thousands right now. But only as we work as a group can we succeed. A lot of healers haven't healed their own pain. But they need to because they have the power to heal the world. The following comes from Jesus through Suzy. "Loving ourselves is a top priority. We need to love ourselves more. Our heart is where we find the answers. Move the intellect out of the way and allow our heart to find the answer. We were born knowing. We can't walk two paths. We are afraid to get on our path because we are so powerful. Some walk in the darkness because it's a lesson and their journey.

Eventually, they get caught up in this darkness and they gain the wrong power. We should be living in gratitude for all the hard lessons we are learning. Say the Lord's Prayer. It holds high vibration."

The energy flowed back and forth between Suzy and Jesus, but the message was very clear. We must love ourselves and remember why we came to earth at this time in history. Using past life regression therapy is one effective way to help us remember why we came to earth.

Suzy told me later that her back pain had almost healed after this session. She has now retired from nursing and is a medium and a psychic for clients full-time.

The message coming from Suzy, as she channeled Jesus, tells us to work in groups to accomplish great changes for the earth. To save it from the destruction which we have caused, we must stand united in care and protection for our treatment of the earth for not only our future, but our children's future.

My dear friend, Patti Osbourne, is a social worker with her own practice as well as assisting at a local hospital in psychological evaluations. She is also a Certified Past Life Regressionist. In May of 2012, Pat served as a channel for her spirit guides, Quan Yin, St. Germain, and Merlin, as I facilitated the flow of information between Patti and her guides.

P: I see myself at the Hall of Mary at Versailles in France. The door opens to gardens. It is spring. I see sculpted shrubs and gravel paths all through a magnificent garden. Now I see St. Germain. He is a slender, elegant man. He has on a 17th century costume. Other people around him are dressed in elegant gowns for the time. Next, I see Merlin. He is dressed in robes, has on a

pointed hat, with his wand, and a long white beard.
Again, I see someone else. It is Quan Yin. The children
are dressed in 17th century clothes. They are playing
and enjoying the day.

L: Is Pat going to find peace in this life for herself?

P: St. Germain speaks: You forget that I am there. In the
     presence of mastery, you are never alone. We watch
     over you. We advise you. Your ego mind tries to rival
     us.

Merlin speaks: "You take things way too seriously. These
     lessons we are sharing with you, you will be using in
     your life in its own time. In other lives, you were a master
     among masters. Forgetting is a way of preservation.
     You do not have to remember. Just connect with the
     tools we give you for growth and for blessings of others.
     We know you have good intentions. The doors have
     swung open to another chapter. You are now ready for
     the conflict between the material and spiritual worlds.
     You are already with us."

Quan Yin speaks: "I hold compassion. I so appreciate your
     holding images of me in your workplace. This is the
     work you are to do: do nothing now. Your place here
     is secure. Merely breathing is all you need to do. You
     are beloved by your lineage. We are graced by your
     attentiveness to your spirituality. You fly to us in your
     sleep. Know that this gentle animal is so loving of you
     and brings in energy for you (Patti's black cat, Spooky).
     His sweetness is how we show ourselves to you. He
     absorbs your energy. You became knowledgeable that
     these animals agree to come back and share lives with
     us. And they are much more important than you know.

They have very important reasons for being with you humans. They have deep love to give."

Quan Yin continues to channel through Patti and say: "We have given you signs. The ego wants to protect you. You will come through this trip (Patti was leaving on a month-long trip to California). This is your opportunity to trust as you ready yourself to cut the ties. "

L: Quan Yin, Patti would like to know about her memory. Could you address her loss of memory?

P: Quan Yin speaks: "Your memory is being changed. You are giving away souvenirs. It's okay. The information you are releasing is unimportant. There is nothing wrong. Your DNA is changing. The plan to go to southern Colorado in the summertime is important. Enjoy that. It is part of your activation. Beings will be around you from other galaxies. They will be supportive of you and earth's changes."

L: Patti would like to know if she is to be a medical intuitive.

P: Quan Yin: "This has been going on for many years. That is why you have been drawn to the hospital setting. You are bringing the energy to the hospital. You can use this to be a healer among healers. We know you feel frustration with the ego at the hospital. You are there and fulfill your contract by being there. You, Linda and Earl, (Linda Backman and her husband, Earl, our Past Life Regression Teacher), Wayne Peterson (author of *Extraordinary Times, Extraordinary Beings*), and you were all in the court together in France in the 17th century (sic) when the French Revolutionary War was going on. Then, the egos of your souls were stripped.

You were all eventually beheaded. But now, you are here in this time together as friends, and it's different. The earth plates are shifting now. Know that you are loved and we are always with you. Be patient with your body. It is wired to make your emotions difficult. But you have a done a good job of balancing these emotions. We show you these beautiful stones on the console to awaken chakras in you. These beautiful colors are to help with the raising of your consciousness. They are the earth's beauty."

St. Germain speaks: "We are so happy to have this voice through you. We understand that to be alone and to meditate is hard for you. Being in a group brings you to a deeper place. We support you in finding these places. Meditating in groups is good for the planet. We want you to know one final thing. Animals evolve through human souls."

In the Buddhist tradition, Quan Yin is the embodiment of compassionate loving kindness. As the Bodhisattva of Compassion, she hears the cries of all beings. Often she is shown pouring a stream of healing water, the "Water of Life," from a small vase. She blesses all living things with physical and spiritual peace.

The Ascended Master Saint Germain is one of the great beings from the Spiritual Hierarchy who govern this system of worlds. He is the cosmic authority under the Seventh Ray, the Violet Ray, the purifying, cleansing power that is raising the Earth into its permanent Golden Age.

The Great White Brotherhood (GWB) is a spiritual organization composed of those ascended masters who have united for the purposes of God in man as set forth by Jesus the Christ, Buddha, and other world leaders. The GWB are releasing the full teachings of cosmic law and are led by Saint Germain. Jesus described them as being "robed in white" in the book of Revelation.

The next case involves the wisdom coming from the Great White Brotherhood. My master guide, Aranthia, and my two most important additional guides, Jonathan and Rhone, are all from the Great White Brotherhood. So naturally, I was very interested in hearing from this group of ascended beings. Any time we can get other-worldly encouragement or information, we should be listening closely.

Patrick Leland is a referred client that I met while doing a group of past life regression sessions in Ft. Myers, Florida. It was May of 2011 when I met Patrick. He told me he wanted to know of his karmic past. The uniqueness of his past life regression is that he was a man in a life in the 1700s in Scotland and as he moved himself into this past life, he took on the brogue of a Scottish accent. Then, as we called in his spirit guides, I was very happy to realize his guides were also from the Great White Brotherhood. I am going to take you directly to the end of the session to learn more about the Great White Brotherhood and what we can expect to learn from the Earth's shift.

L: Now please ask your spirit guides to come through and tell us about the Great White Brotherhood.

P: It's a very big group. They are like one voice. There is no separate spokesman. I am asking them the name they would like to be called.

Patrick's demeanor changed and he started talking in a strong voice that was not his soft, clear one. The voice seemed very confident, strong, and commanding.

GWB: "We understand you like the Great White Brotherhood!"
      (Of course, as the facilitator, I was very excited to know

I was among the ascended masters of the GWB because my spirit guides were also from this group of masters.)

GWB: "We do not marry.... We have shown Patrick several past lives in the past. We knew him then in Scotland. We worked with him even then. The female was very connected to spirit, an imprint, as it were. It was a very intricate life. There was much planning that went into Patrick's life to bring him to this time and place he is in today in the present. There will be no chance that this will fail. There are some that will claim this life and some that will fail. This path has been set for many lifetimes. This is as much about earth as his home planet. He is to observe and report. His planet appears in shades of purple and yellow. The bodies of the beings on his planet are not as Earth. There is no body, only spirit (or soul). Lifetimes are very long. There is a connectedness between all spirits there. Their chakras are arranged differently. They are not connected to the emotional body as humans are."

P: Will I return to earth again after this life?

GWB: "You enjoy your planet and the toys. You were sent to observe and report. The future and the past are simply structures on your planet. It might amuse you to know that what you think is the future is more present than you think. You (Earth) are closing many doors. You are folding the laundry. We prefer to think of it in the term, "Gaining Experience." It's all there and it's all treasure. Always remember that we are right by you. It's a time of opening, although it seems a time of closing. Technology is helping. Limbs can move by technology, etc. It's a planet of evolution, this Earth. It's accelerating. Human lifetimes will be much longer."

GWB: "Every time we meet, Patrick is speechless. You know the formula, Patrick."

L: May I ask you, The Great White Brotherhood, about my guides? Their names are Aranthia and Rhone.

GWB: They are the spark guys!

This had a very personal meaning to me. During this time, my spirit guides sent electromagnetic light energy to me. It continued for several months, and my hands were unable to control the rise in light energy. I destroyed my satellite receiver box and remote and I had to replace it. My hands made my mouse to my computer inoperable and even my curling iron, hair dryer and cell phone would not work properly. My watch would not work for days. Yet, after days of having it off, it would resume working. I had been giving classes at a metaphysical store in Colorado Springs on this very topic, "Effects of the Ascension Process."

GWB: They are in shades of aqua and purple. You have a third guide. (I now know the guide as Jonathan. I had thought he was in my soul group as a guide, but had not realized until this session that he, too, was from the GWB.)

L: Thank you so much, GWB, for this enlightening information.

When we left the session, both Patrick and I knew something very incredible had happened to both of us. Patrick asked what exactly had happened in the session. He knew he had channeled ascended beings. He tried to describe the process to me. When I asked a question, he could feel that there were several beings trying to answer the question. Energy would come to his mind from several different directions and then it would become focused into one voice for the group. He was quite amazed at the information, as was I. Yet, the Great White Brotherhood and other ascended beings are more than eager to help us with this transformation of our world. We just need to remember to ask them to come through to communicate with us during meditation or prayer or in our dream state.

Let's discuss for a moment the simple way to meditate to bring through our spirit guides and ascended beings. I use a very simple process that just takes a little time and some basic practice. In our busy lives today, it may seem hard to find a quiet few moments alone to go within. But all you need is a corner spot or a private sofa in a room. Some even go outside on a delightful patio. No more than twenty to thirty minutes of meditative time will allow one to connect with their higher soul self and with their spirit guides.

I have several relaxing scenes I call to memory when I want to communicate with my guides. These scenes can be of walking in a beautiful meadow, feeling the grass against your legs as the wind blows it, and hearing the birds singing in the trees nearby, plus seeing the butterflies as they land on the wildflowers in the meadows. Cross over a beautiful stream with grassy banks on either side, and then look ahead at a gorgeous cliff or a serene forest ahead. Here you can stop and contemplate what you want to say to your guides.

I also see my seven chakras and their colors. I go through a clearing process with each one of the chakras before I go to the forest or cliff. This allows the light channel from your higher self to be totally cleared for best results.

If you know your spirit guides' names, simply ask them to come through for you and give you signs, words, understanding and insight in how best to be of service to your fellow man. I also ask how do I best stay on my chosen soul's path. Then just go within and be still. Let the grocery list pass by your view, the errands you need to do drop away, and sit quietly.

Soon, you will begin to feel a presence around you. There might be one or several of your guides and family members from the other side who come close to you. Staying still, simply be. What may come through for you next are feelings, understanding, and spiritual uplifting. These thoughts and feelings are your spirit guides and ascended beings communicating with you. Please take a journal with you and be sure to write down anything you hear or feel afterward. Your spirit guides will be so happy that you called on them. That is their job and that is how they can aid you in your journey.

Marlena Patton is a well-known psychic and medical intuitive in southern Florida and we have known each other for over twelve years. Yet, not until May, 2011, would we have our first opportunity for a PLR session together. The lives she experienced were meaningful to her, but what was so very enlightening to me were the messages her ascended master guides had for her and me that day. One of her past lives was as a Native American. The Indian chief in her past life now comes through as one of her spirit guides as well as others who come.

M: The Indian chief in the past life is one of my spirit guides. He is very tall, strong, and handsome. Sometimes he wears a big feather headdress and sometimes he wears a bear headdress on his head. His name is Big Bear. He comes around me a lot. I see three beings from the hood group of guides (Great White Brotherhood). I see no feet. They won't show me features. The whole group is here.

L: Guides, would you please tell Marlena her soul's purpose in this present life?

GWB: To be one of the 144,000. The Melchizedek Group. Your purpose is to transform darkness into light. The readings, healings, and night work you do while your body sleeps are all a part of this. You are working very hard to clear negative energy. At night you leave and go to the astral plane to save people. You help them in transitioning to home. You are doing a good job, the group say. This is why you are so tired. When Jesus healed others, he was very tired.

L: Who with Marlena now is part of her soul group?

GWB: Very few. Her mother, father, brother, and her children have all been with her in past lives.

L: Does Marlena have spirit attachments?

GWB: Yes, she has them. We are working on removing them and we have already cleared her aura.

L: What is in the future for Marlena?

GWB: She will be working with a group of us. There is new hearing work. She will be working directly with us. The "Grapefruit Orbs" take her to the astrals and return her home. You are from two different groups. The Arcturians and the Arkuthremaims(Sp?). Your guides will be giving you information. Write it down. Share it only with a small group. It transmutes darkness. They will know what to do with this. On Earth and in another space. It's hidden now. In about a month, it will be revealed to you. A lot of change. Lee will be working some with Marlena. Marlena is loved very much by our group....She gets the tough assignments. She is not coming back after this life. She rarely comes around. It's necessary for her to be here for the planetary shift.

L: We would like to ask about Marlena's children.

GWB: They will be fine. They will remember. Big Bear is your master guide.

L: Marlena would like to know if she works with Jesus.

GWB: Marlena always works with the Christ Consciousness.

L: Is Marlena from Arcturus originally?

GWB: Yes and no. There is a connection, but she comes from a different place now. She comes from the north. It's completion. She is completing her soul's path. She works with a very big group with the White Eagle making very big plans. She goes from place to place to hold vibrations.

L: Since my guides are with the GWB also, could you confirm for me that I am also from Arcturus?

GWB: Energetically yes, but physically, you are from Texas!

Lee: Very Funny!... Could I ask a few questions about the planetary shift? Will we be able to do so many of the things people are predicting about the future after the shift?

GWB: You will be able to see your guides more clearly as the veil thins. You will be able to telecommunicate with each other. For Lee to better receive the message from your guides, you need to work on quieting your mind. It will help in your work. You need to purify your emotions. Yes, there will be more people leaving the planet from disasters.

Lee: Are our governmental and economic systems changing in the near future?

GWB: No.... Marlena's guides will be rewiring her body for her work ahead so that she will be better able to handle the many tasks she will be undertaking in the future.

The history of the planet, Arcturus, that Marlena's guides said she originated from, is that it is the brightest star in the constellation Bootes. It is a relatively close star at only 36.7 light-years from Earth, and, together with Vega and Sirius, one of the most luminous stars in the Sun's neighborhood. It has likely exhausted its hydrogen and has begun fusing helium into oxygen and carbon in its core. It will continue to expand before sloughing off its outer shell and ending its life (Wikipedia). The second planet, Arkuthremaims, has not been identified in any of the reference sources.

Once again, the ascended beings gave us new information about the coming shift of the Earth and what the ascension process has in store for us all. We need to take the advice the GWB gave to me and apply it to the entire planet. We need to work to silence our minds of the "white noise" so that we can connect more to our Spirit Guides who are always there to help us when we are ready to hear them. And we could all be helped by "purifying our emotions." Instead of being anxious about all the changes we see and feel happening all around us, we should work toward group efforts to help the planet. Only in oneness will we be able to use our strength to its greatest potential to help Mother Gaia as she births a "New Earth."

Agoraphobia, or the fear of open spaces, and panic attacks are psychological phobias that are debilitating to the individual experiencing them. It is widely recognized that incidents in one's current life set the stage for these types of phobias. However, our past life may also hold a key to understanding current fears and anxiety disorders. Past life regression therapy may be the effective tool that takes a client's higher self back to the trauma of a prior life. Through a past life regression, the current phobia can then be released.

In October of 2011, Polly Grayson, a client who suffered with agoraphobia, wanted to use past life regression to free her from its hold. Polly is a perky, attractive wife and mother of three children in her early 40s, but she was hiding a dark secret. She was afraid to leave her home. Rarely would she leave for any reason and she could not understand why. She felt there had been nothing in her present life to warrant such a life-limiting reaction. Polly believed that her emotional feelings were coming from past life experiences. We agreed that I might be able to help her.

In Polly's light trance, she enters a life where she sees a young girl named Michelle.

L: What year do you feel you are experiencing?

P: It is 1408.

L: Can you tell me the name of the young girl?

P: Her name is Michelle. She has on black buckled shoes. She is wearing leotards and a plaid dress that comes to her knees. She has her hair in a ponytail.

L: Do you recognize her soul essence as anyone you know in Polly's life today?

P: Yes, she is my niece, Angela.

L: What do you see next?

P: I see that she is happy but she is snooty. She's a spoiled little girl. She has servants around her. Next I see myself walking up to the mansion where Michelle is. I am her grandmother, Lidia, and I am supposed to take care of her. But I see that Michelle has slipped away from the servants and she has found a gun and it has gone off. It killed her! I am supposed to protect her from any harm! I am looking inside the mansion but I can't get in. The doors are locked. I am frantic. I see the little girl inside but I can't get to her. I feel that I have just lost everything. I am lying down now like I am going to die. I die right there. I was supposed to be watching her, but I left and the little girl grabbed a gun. I die right there from the anxiety of leaving her alone.

P: I know that Michelle's mother died when she was born. The father, my son, was away when it happened. He had everything of his removed before the baby Michelle came home. He now lives in another country.

L: Do you recognize the soul essence of the father, your son, today in Polly's life?

P: Yes, he is my Uncle Ray.

L: Please go on.

P: He never came back. He just sent money to take care of Michelle, the little girl. I, as the grandmother, was to keep her safe and love her. It is really desolate here. No one is going to find me (Lidia) outside the mansion.

As quickly as her life ended, Polly moved directly into another life led by her spirit guides. The scene has her running very quickly.

P: I am running from someone. I am a little boy about 12 years old. I am in an old Western town in 1892.

L: Can you tell me your name?

P: My name is Darryl. It's 1892, and I am running from a saloon. I have stolen something and I have to feed my family with what I have stolen. I have suspenders on. I am running toward my family's home. I am running up a hill. I am running and running. All of a sudden, I reach a cliff and I can't stop and I fall off the cliff. It kills me.

L: It's okay. You will feel no pain at falling off the cliff.

P: I see my mom waiting with two smaller siblings at home for me.

L: Do you recognize the soul essence of your mother as anyone you know today in Polly's life?

P: Yes, she is my Grandma Owens. I don't recognize the two siblings. They look like twins. My mom is strange. She doesn't talk to anyone. She's uptight. The boys are

James and Tom. We stayed away from town because my mom was a crazy type. She believed differently. She talks to the moon. And no one wants to help her. She tries to live off the land. The town doesn't like her. I hope the boys have enough food to eat.

L: Whenever you are ready, Polly, release your soul from your body as the little boy, Darryl, and slowly move above the scene and rise up into the clouds to open yourself to your complete higher soul self. On the count of three, I ask you to bring in your spirit guides to tell us more about these two past lives they have shown you.

P: I see "Mohow." He is my Native American spirit guide. Mohow says to start a clean sheet. I have to make my own life now. I need to erase the memories of these two past lives.

L: Ask your spirit guide why you were shown these two lives.

P: I can protect all I want, they tell me. Yet, it is going to happen the way it is going to happen. I want to control. I have to stop being so paranoid about the children (Polly's three children). I need to let go. They will protect themselves. Let go. Let go.

L: Ask your master guide what your path today is.

P: I see me working with women to meditate. I see a meditation room. Mohow says not to focus on it. It is coming. It's a healing house. It's a secret house. It's a meditation room and a reading room. It's just found by word of mouth. It is not advertised. There are four of us there helping in the meditation.

P: Once again, I hear let go, let go, let go. I am going to be all right. They are with me all the time. My guides are smiling. They have plans for me. They say I can't know everything yet. The meditation house is going to be beautiful. It's an old-fashioned church. They say I will be meeting people soon to connect to who will be involved in the meditation house.

Polly contacted me a few days later to tell me how excited she was. She could feel a huge release happening. She no longer feared leaving her home. She was talking to her children. She assured them she would no longer be so worried when they went out of the house. (In the past she had worried constantly when any of her children were gone.) The two past lives had been frightening for her. As Lidia, the grandmother, she had not been able to protect the little granddaughter, Michelle, from accidentally shooting herself. As Darryl, she had not been able to protect or provide for her two little brothers. Now she understood why she had always felt a need to be at home at all times for her children. She never wanted them to come home to an empty house.

Polly knew that she had turned a corner in her destiny for the better. She told me she now had confidence about the future. She no longer felt trapped in her own house.

> A common feature in past-life research is that symbols from a prior lifetime are found in the person's contemporary incarnation and synchronistic events occur which seem to reinforce past life connections.[10]

---

[10] Walter Semkiw, MD., *Born Again, Reincarnation Cases Involving International Celebrities India's Political Legends And Film Stars*, (New Delhi, India, 110024: Ritana Books, 2006), 34.

In April of 2012, Janice Rainey was a staff person in a metaphysical book store in Colorado Springs where I conducted classes. She suffered from panic attacks. She had resigned herself to the thought that a family move when she was 12 was the origin of the phobia. There was the new school, the new classmates, and the new friends that she was challenged with when she moved to a new state. But as time went on, the panic attacks only increased in their intensity. Between 19 and 23 years of age, she additionally suffered from agoraphobia. Now in her early 40s, she was recently remarried and very happy. However, the panic attacks had never gone away. Janice felt that the cause must be something beyond the original shift in her young life of moving to Colorado. Together, we hoped to discover the cause through the PLR work. Janice's opening scene was that of a large tree.

J: I am in front of a large tree. I can see the bark on the tree and the tree has a hole in the middle. I hear water running. I "feel" like there is foliage all around and it feels very enclosed where I am. I feel like I am here, but I am not here. Buried-----I am buried in front of the big tree. I see now that there is a fresh mound of dirt in front of the tree. I am buried in that hole in front of the tree, and I am buried alive!

J: Below the ground, I am a young girl, about 11 to 12 years of age. I can see her. She looks so much like a fairy figurine I just purchased because I was so drawn to it. She has long brown hair. Her dress is tattered, however. She fought her attacker.

L: Can you tell us what country you are in and what year it is?

J: It's Germany and the year is 1717. My name is Jane. I
      am scared. A man put me down here. My uncle put me
      here. I am feeling so much rage, hate, and jealousy. I
      don't understand. I was born out of wedlock and was
      hidden by my mother. I couldn't be known to anyone.

L: Please go on and tell us more of what you see and know
      about little Jane.

J: My mother had me because my uncle sexually assaulted
      my mother. He was married to someone else. My mother
      was very young when she got pregnant with me. My
      mother was hidden by my uncle. When I came along, I
      had to hide, too. I couldn't play outside. I had no partner
      to play with, I had to hide all the time. Mom was sad. I
      tried to make Mom happy, but I couldn't. My mom was
      ashamed. She couldn't accept me. Mom helped bury
      me! My uncle was abusive. His name was John. I am so
      tense! I was in the corner. I could hear them planning
      to put me underground. I am an abomination. My mom
      was raped by my uncle. She never wanted me.

J: Why did they wait until I was 12 to kill me? My uncle
      wasn't around for a big part of our lives. Then the
      menses came. It was dirty. We were Quakers. Lust was
      the reason he raped my mother. She was pretty. She
      feared he would do the same to me. In her heart, she
      loved me. It caused her a lot of grief to kill me.

J: ......I see John at the edge of the bed. He has on dirty
      clothes and a grey beard. He scared me. When he
      started to stare at me, I would scream. Then he would
      disappear. I see a shack in the woods. She never took
      Jane (Janice) anywhere. Mom was in fear, fear, fear.

L: Please tell me what happened as Jane grew up.

J: I tried to be a good little girl. The uncle had put my mother in the shack. Her parents had passed. No one missed her. He took her to the shack and no one missed her. It went on for a while. She was in his care. His wife knew what he was doing and she helped.

L: Do you recognize the soul essence of the wife of John?

J: Yes, it is my Grandmother Cramer. My mom was 20. I watched him rape her. I was between a bedpost and the wall. My hands were over my ears and I was singing to drown out the sounds of her screaming. My mom had fear that he would rape me as well. She had to save me. Her baby girl. It was no life. She knew it was coming. He would rape me soon. My mom faked my death. I drank something that was bitter and I got sleepy. (Janine says it was poisonous berries.) My uncle was told by my mother that I was dead, and he dug the hole to bury me.

L: Who in your present life is the soul essence of your mother in Jane's life?

J: I see that it's my sister, Melissa, who was my mother in this past life as Jane.

L: Please tell us what you see next.

J: I see my mom just crying over the mound. I think she thought I would fall asleep and die in the grave. I see her lying across the mound and crying. But I wake up in the grave! I didn't understand what had happened. I couldn't move. It is so vivid. I was so scared and it was so dark. I am sick to my stomach (the poisonous berries). I am trying to get my head up and I can't. No air. I can't move.

L: Please tell us what you see next. You will not feel any pain as you slowly drift off from not being able to breath.

J: My mom went into a depression. The raping by my uncle was still going on. She was sickly and she didn't live much longer. She starved herself to death. I remember I was always trying to be as pretty as she was as I was growing up in the woods. She was spiritual. My mom was tormented and picked on as a child after her parents died. She rather liked my uncle's attention at first. She wanted to be loved. Then he started raping her. Her parents died of a sickness. She took care of them until they died.

L: Do you recognize the soul essence of the parents as anyone you know in Janice's life today?

J: Yes, they are my parents today.

L: Janice, please ask your spirit guides to join us and let us know more about the past life you just experienced on the count of three. One, two, and three.

J: I feel hands on my shoulders. My grandparents are here. My Grandpa and Grandma are saying that Michael is giving you strength. There is a statue of Archangel Michael that I look at often in the store. The energy of Archangel Michael is helping me heal. He is my master guide.......I next see one that gives me my sense of humor. "I am a hot dog" he says. It's Maxi, a dog. He gives me unconditional love. He is the soul essence of my dog, Otis, that Justin, my new husband, just gave me. Maxi had Justin give me Otis as a gift after a hard time we both just went through when Justin lost his job as a plumber after his company downsized. Recently, Justin has found a new job and we are getting back to normal, but this period was anxiety-ridden for me. I have always felt that Otis was more than just a dog. I am also seeing a child as well. I miscarried at 3 months long ago. But my spirit guides are telling me I am not ready to meet the child today. They will wait until I am stronger.

This young Jane was so panic-stricken in her past life recalling events that I sensed from my guides that it was not the time to ask her who the uncle was in her present life. Maybe a second session, after Janice had regained confidence about this past life and her capabilities to re-experience the connection. The soul essence of the uncle may not even be in her present life. She did later tell me that her sister, Melissa, had been told about this past life. Melissa wants to experience a past life recall, herself, in the near future to glean even more awakening for both her and her sister, Janice.

This session was emotional for Janice and for me as well. To feel the pain of an innocent young girl being so traumatized is hard for anyone to accept. Many days later in the store, I asked Janice how she was doing. She said she immediately felt lighter and happier after the regression. She had noticed that when events come up that would normally have sent her into a panic attack in the past, she is able to handle them more calmly today and does not lose her emotional control over the situation as she once did.

These two cases involved traumatic events in the souls' past lives. Our higher soul selves believe that we can overcome traumatic events such as these and grow stronger as a result. However, humans experience fear and anxiety differently than an evolved soul does when it is in spirit. Experiences of fear and anxiety cause humans to develop karma that is reconciled in future lives. Phobias, psychological disorders, physical reactions and depression propel fearful emotions to the surface of our personality. Past life regression therapy serves as a key to unlock and release the anxiety and fear called into one's current life by revisiting the past in a safe and guided place when the emotional scenes from the past surface. Now Polly and Janice have a chance to more fully complete their spiritual paths in their present lives.

CHAPTER NINE
PAST LIVES AS ELEMENTALS AND FAIRIES

> Life blossoms into abundance
> covering the earth with its grandeur.
> Nature and man serve a common destiny;
> nurturing the Planet with love.
> *Meredith Lady Young*[11]

Elementals and fairies have been in folklore and ancient tales for centuries. Regardless of how you feel about the existence of the elementals and fairies, please read the following cases with an open mind. Over a period of three years of doing past life regression cases in Colorado, I repeatedly worked with clients who had previous lives in fairy realms or were told by their spirit guides that they had once had lifetimes as an elemental. Fiona Murray from Scotland explains elementals and fairies on her website, www.elementalbeings.co.uk:

> "Fairies are the most commonly known Elemental, probably because fairies are everywhere. They are the guardians of plants and flowers. Every plant has a Fairy on it or even more than one. Elementals

---

[11] Meredith Lady Young, *Agartha*, (Walpole, NH: Stillpoint Publishing, 1984), Page 223.

are otherwise known as nature spirits or
guardians. Elementals reside all over the
world. They are, I believe, what gives many
of the great wildernesses of the world that
magical feeling that is hard to describe until
one has felt if for themselves. They are the
reason one feels more peaceful and relaxed
if sitting under a tree, by a river, on a beach or
in a grass meadow." 12

From what the spirit guides tell us in these regressions,
our world will be connecting once again to the fairy and
elemental realms in a physical way in our near future.
Maybe that is why so many sessions have shown up at this
time to pass along to others the understanding of the fairy
and elemental realm now. We can start communicating
with their energy in the present to prepare us for physical
connection in the future.

Rebecca Crider is a cheery young woman who gives
off a sparkly quality of energy which is palpable when just
standing next to her. Rebecca saw two lives in a past life
regression session with me. The first life was of a young
slave at the age of 12 named Greta, in Alabama in 1706. She
did not understand being controlled by her master (the
white owner). She eventually tried to marry, but the master
killed her husband before they could marry, telling her that
she could not be married and be a slave. He then went on to
rape her. She lived out the rest of her days as an obedient
slave. She saw that the master was her mother, Shirley, today
and her husband-to-be in 1706 was her son, Freddy, in her
present life.

---

12 Fiona Murray, www.elementalbeings.co.uk, (Scotland,
    viewed July 4, 2012).

The second life starts with the scene at twilight.

R: It's twilight. There are lots of trees and I am in a forest. The fairies, they know me. I am barefoot. I have bare legs. I have on a tattered skirt. I am benevolent, but feel irritation. I have on a shawl and I am old, like a crone. I have a fair face with wrinkles. The fairies are telling me that I am a fairy goddess on the inside, but that I shapeshift to look like a crone. It is the 1400s but I am several hundred years old. I have a limitless age. I protect the forest. They bring me food and herbs. They are excited. I have been gone to the village. Fairies are tiny and twiggy-like. They have flesh but it is pointy. And they have leaves growing out of the skin. They have tufts of hair and it is fluffy and chestnut in color. They have knitted little hats on. They are all wearing hats. "Brownie" is my son Freddy. Brownie is like a monkey-size. There are hundreds of them. Then there are the bird-size fairies. They are different breeds. There are many different breeds of fairies. They come in many different sizes and shapes. Then there is the Council. They are very tall, about seven feet in height. They are ancient like angels. The Council members come in all colors of the chakras. They are blue, green, pink, orange and all of the chakra colors. The colors pulsate on their bodies. Each color represents a separate chakra on them, and all the chakras make a ping sound as they pulsate up and down their bodies.

R: I am a messenger. I am the link to the human world. My name is Raysha. There are the trees that are not trees. They are twig-like and stand against a tree and become part of the tree (elementals). They do the same with air and water. I see a man, Ravener, and I see him shapeshift. It is around the time of Camelot but before Merlin was known as Merlin. It was a time before Arthur became King. We know of him coming. He gives us hope. King Arthur does. Things are wrong. Our Council is meeting. This man, Ravener, came from the darker part of the forest. He works as a link as I do. There are many of us. There is a link throughout the world with other fairies, and elementals.

L: Please move now to the next most important scene in this past life you are experiencing on the count of three. One, two, three.

R: I am sitting at a fire. There is a castle in the distance. I am waiting on an answer. I am waiting to know if I am to proceed with a project or not. I am using good magic with crystals and smoke, caused by the herbs in the fire. The crystals are in the fire. They do not crack. I am trying to strengthen the earth. So much blood has defiled the planet. I am chanting a verse over and over. The fire opens and the earth takes the crystals. Each crystal is a different energy. There are so many souls being killed. It is painful for earth. I go everywhere earth is holding the pain. I am helping Mother Earth to release the pain. Also, there is much disease. I am renewing the ground. Many like me are doing this. It is a worldwide link. This ceremony releases the form of the human for Raysha. Now I see that all changes before my eyes. I am now a fairy goddess again. The fairies recede into dormancy. They are still there. They hate concrete. They are now in the rocks. They have become pure energy. At certain times of the earth, they still come out. Their freedom was taken. They lost their forests. They are nomads. They feel like they lost their homes. I see Raysha holding her hand out to me. What you believe is real. I am still with you and part of you.

L: I ask Rebecca to bring in her spirit guides to give us more information on these lives she was shown, on the count of three. One, two, three.

R: There is a very strong male here. His name is Paul. He is irritated with me. He has a sense of humor. He has a beard and darker hair. He is Irish or Scottish. He is chunky and beefy. He has a big leather strap across his chest. He has boots, dark brown pants on and a red nose. He likes his drink. He comes and picks me up. "Come on," he says, "get moving. Roscha is here."

R: She is tall with wavy hair and conical hat on like a wizard. She has gem crystals on her chakra points and she is waving her arms. She has shiny iridescent skin and big eyes. Akasha is here. She is like a twin soul for me. She gets me. She gets my humanness. Paul is saying "It's your choice." Life is making me sad. Paul says, "You don't need to be sad. It's not going to get much better (Rebecca asked about her marriage). You need to see that." I can't share this with him, the mystical side.

L: Can Paul enlighten us on why the life as a black slave maid was experienced?

R: Paul says that no one is my master. I cannot be my true self if I let someone control me. If one does this, the soul suffers. I have forgotten who I was as a fairy goddess because I am being oppressed in life after life. The slave life and now in this life by my husband. The master is an illusion. In this life, there is no master. Your made your husband your master. You need to find your passion. Act on your talents. I paint and I write. My spirit guide Paul says, "Get moving."

I believe Rebecca's guides said it all. She is to use her mystical spirit side more in this life to bring light to others and to herself. She mentioned that she has fairy décor and figurines everywhere in her home. They are part of who she is and she will only be fulfilled in this life if and when she begins using the creative and magical side of her true soul essence.

I met Leslie Chisholm back in the summer of 2010 at a group past life regression session I was giving. She later called for a one-on-one past life regression to find answers to burning questions about herself she had had all her adult life. She asked about these concerns as we began the interview session before the regression. "I would like to know why people do not hear me," she said. She also felt her life was very difficult and that she worked so hard for everything she had. She felt that her life was very limiting. She also wondered why her son was so estranged from her. I thought we would find the answers to these questions in a past life where she had not shown enough determination to make a success of her life. But I was in for a very different experience with Leslie.

Leslie: It's warm and I am outside. It looks like a fairyland as I look around. There are birds everywhere singing. There is a lovely stream, and the colors of everything are so vibrant. The colors are much more brilliant than anything in life on this planet. Fairies, like Tinkerbell, are greeting me and telling me welcome back. They are very tiny. They are coming closer now and touching me. They are happy to see me. I get the sense that they know me. I can feel the breeze against my face. It's a nice, soft environment.

Lee: Please describe what you are wearing.

Leslie: My shoes are pointed and white. They glitter and at the point there is a white stone. The shoes have heels. My dress is blue. It has a sweetheart neckline. It has sleeves, and they are chiffon. The dress is full and loose. I have on a gold necklace with big pearls on it. I have beautiful blonde upswept hair. I am very dainty with a cute, turned up nose. I am in my 20s. But I feel I might really be many hundreds of years old........

Leslie: I am much bigger than anyone else in the forest. Every other creature is tiny. I have a unicorn by my side and he nuzzles me. We have a bond with each other. My name starts with a "B." Beyond the stream is a hill and a grassy meadow. There is a cottage. That is my home. I know it to be my home. (Linda starts crying.) I am now walking over the wooden bridge to my cottage. The unicorn is walking with me and I have my hand on his back. The cottage is yellow with white trim and it has flower boxes under the windows. There is a white rocking chair on the front porch and the front door is a white Dutch door with the top half open.

Leslie: I am feeling tears of joy to be home again! The house is tiny and it has a rock fireplace. It has a kitchen and a very antique stove that I do not know how to cook on as I look at it. The home has hardwood floors. I live there by myself. I am alone in the world except for the creatures and the fairies of the forest. I feel there is no family. There is a wise old man that is my friend. He lives beyond the hill. He is my guide. He's a wizard and he is very old. He is many hundreds of years old. He is grey and very wrinkled, but very wise.

Leslie: I am the guide and the protector of the forest. I know that I make delicious buns that all the fairies love. They want me to make some now. I see that the home has French doors and the windows are hinged to swing out.

Lee: Can you tell me where you are?

Leslie: It's the land of King Arthur, the round table and all.

Lee: Did you know King Arthur?

Leslie: He was a man of vision. Merlin is the old man wizard that I saw earlier. I was as powerful as Merlin, my guides are telling me. My job was to watch over the fairies and the forest.

Lee: What about Avalon?

Leslie: The women of Avalon were naïve, and idealistic. They thought they could change the world. During this life I felt very content and happy and loving. I was wanted by everyone in the forest.

Lee: Let's now move to the next most important scene in this past life on the count of three. One, two three.

Leslie: It's dark and cold and windy. It's all gone! There is a big black cloud.

Lee: What happened?

Leslie: A man with the first initial of "M" caused the big black cloud. He burned everything. There is no harm to the fairies. (Then Leslie hands me a fairy with her palm out to me as if the fairy were standing on it.) Here is Guine, she says. (pronounced "Gwen"). Her home is gone now. All the flowers are gone. I had to find a new place to live. I found a cave and an underground pool with blue water and white light in it. But winter is coming and I have no food. I then die.

Lee: Now rise above your body and be ready to say goodbye to anyone that you love.

Leslie: It is better that I died than to have stayed and have lived like that. Better than to have experienced the meanness that was to follow. But I feel bad because I let the forest creatures down. It was my job to keep them safe. They all went to a world that you can't see.

Lee: It was not your fault and there was nothing you could have done to prevent the violence to the forest. There were many battles around the time King Arthur.

Leslie: I just want to say goodbye to the wizard and thank him for all that he did for me.

Lee: Now I ask you to bring through your spirit guides on the count of three so we can ask for more insight into this past life for you. One, two, three.

Leslie: Agatha is here. She has short twisty curls. She is in her mid-thirties. She just tells it like it is. Next I see Mike. He has dark hair, and he is Mediterranean and Roman looking. He seems very deep and thoughtful. He is a philosopher. The rest are here but they are in a group and not willing to identify themselves individually. They feel like fun, laughter, joy, love and bright light.

Lee: What are you doing now?

Leslie: I am floating with my guides.

Lee: Ask you guides why they showed you the fairy priestess life.

Leslie: Because that is who she is, they say. For many, many years, it was my job. Will I go back to that type of life again? They say that I have to heal from the destructive end that I experienced before I died. My guides are saying that I have to believe that I was that fairy priestess first. The fairies are all waiting for me.

Lee: Why do people in this life not hear Leslie?

Leslie: They do not hear her because she does not want to be heard.

Lee: Why is Leslie's life so difficult?

Leslie: I am punishing myself for that trauma that the forest experienced.

Lee: Leslie says she recently dreamed about the 7 dwarfs.

Leslie: We are trying to reach you in your dreams.

Lee: What about her son?

Leslie: He gave up the magic to come into this present life as my son. He had been the unicorn. My guides tell me that I struggle with him because my higher soul self wants him to believe in magic. He can't do that yet, my guides say. He will come around in time, they say. My guides say that I need to look on the other side of myself. I need to acknowledge the truth. I need to stop hiding my life under a bushel. They say that I glow. There is a price to pay for everything, they say. I do not feel guilt or shame. But if people saw how happy, how much joy I felt in that life, I feel I would be hurt again.

Lee: I ask Leslie to move up into the upper realms to her higher soul self.

Leslie: In "Heaven" everyone is little sparks and you can fly. There is joy. There is no ground or sky. You can have a face if you want.

Lee: Is there anything else you want to ask your spirit guides?

Leslie: Why can't I hear you? Because you don't want to, they say. I shut a gate to that life. My guides want me to know to be careful. Not everyone believes in fairies. Not everyone believes in "radiance." I feel a warm cloak around me as the guides are hugging me as they leave. They say be proud of who I am and they love me in spite of what my job is at this time during the shift of the planet. As much as I am afraid of it, I need to shine my radiance. This means to shine my inner light. I would scare many if I showed my full radiance. They say to practice glowing. The people will feel it subconsciously.

For Leslie this was an awakening to feelings she had kept buried for a long, long time (King Arthur was a legendary British leader in the 6th century). This previous life over the fairy realm explained why she was never free to be herself. Her memories are that she would have been punished and killed for it. Now, she could unearth her lightness, her radiance for all to feel and see once and for all.

In May of 2012, I met with Regina Wheeler for a past life regression. She simply wanted to know what many of us want to know. She had trouble finding someone to connect with in a personal relationship in her life. She began seeing a very ordinary past life in the 1600s in Ireland, but as we ventured deeper into the relationship she had with certain members of this past life, what was unveiled was quite interesting.

R: I am outside in the meadow with a forest ahead of me. There is a little cottage ahead covered with ivy.

L: Will you describe what you are wearing?

R: I am barefoot. I can feel the grass under my feet. I have on britches with a leather corset. I have on my brother's shirt underneath the corset. It is beige. I have black hair and it's long.

L: How old are you and what country are you in?

R: I am 18 years old and my name is Jezebel. I am in Ireland and the year is 1634. I am at the cottage. I open the door and I tell everyone hello. I have two little brothers. They are twins and they are four years old.

L: Do you recognize either one of your brothers as anyone you know in your present life?

R: One of them is my best friend today, Scott. I do not recognize the other one. I see my mom, Irene, and I know that I love her.

L: Please tell me if she resonates as anyone you know in your current life.

R: She is one of my friends, Lillie. Irene is cooking dinner. My dad comes in. He's very strict. But he is strict for the best reasons.

L: Do you recognize his soul essence as anyone you know as Regina?

R: I do not recognize him as anyone I know today.........I try to convince Mom to let me go outside, but she says I must feed the twins. I am waiting for Tommy. He is 26 years old. I run up and hug him. He hugs me back. He laughs. He is a farmer. He is my brother. I recognize him as a cousin of mine in my life today. I try to make Tom tell Mom to let me come to Tom's. Tom used to be married. She ran away. He has a little girl who stays with Nana. Nana is a lady we took in and she takes care of the baby.

L: Do you recognize any of them in your present life today?

R: The little girl is Morgan, my sister's second child. I don't recognize Nana. Mom will let me go with Tommy. I like to hide in the forest from him. I run through the trees. He gets worried. He hears thunder. I think it's fun, and I hide in a tree. He keeps calling and I start to get scared. If it gets dark, the animals come out. I call for Tommy. It starts to rain and we cannot hear each other and I can hear wolves nearby. I see Tommy's dog. I start to climb down, and I know that I am safe with him. He leads me out of the forest. I see Tommy's house. I start running toward the door. I see Nana with the baby. Tommy can take care of himself. I sit down and eat. Nana fusses over me. I am going to geta chill if I don't change.

L: On the count of three, please move to the next most important scene in this past life. One, two, three.

R: Detrich walks in. He is Tommy's best friend.

L: Do you recognize Detrich as anyone you know in your
      present life?

R: Yes, he is my boyfriend, Devon. Detrich picks me up
      and throws me. He thinks of me as a puppy. Detrich
      convinces me to go to town. He wants to meet his
      buddies. I go in the pubs.

R: I try to stay near Detrich. There is a brawl in front of
      me. I stay to watch. One of them runs into me. This
      makes Detrich mad. Detrich goes after him. I try to
      stop them. He stops, but says not to tell Tommy. I want
      to leave. He wants to stay. He says that he will keep
      me safe. They are talking about getting into trouble in
      town. I want to leave. Detrich is drunk. I help him to
      the door. Tommy rushes in and takes Detrich outside.
      We head back home. I get to stay at Tommy's house. I
      hear tapping on the window. It's girls from town. They
      want to know about Tommy. They want me to hang out
      with them. They want to play a prank on Mrs. O'Reilly.
      Her husband died and no one knows why. They think
      she's a witch. They throw fruit and bread at her house.
      She shouts to leave and the girls run.

R: I stay behind. I feel bad. I help her clean up. She invites
      me inside. I want to learn about the herbs. She says I am
      too young. She looks like someone, but I'm not close to
      them. I sniff all the plants. Mrs. O'Reilly asks if my mom
      knows I am gone. I lie and say yes. I wander around her
      house. She's making a potion for another mother for her
      pregnancy. I finally leave. I must go through the forest.
      I don't like going through the forest. But I do get home. I
      am covered in mud. I take a dip in the pond.

L: Please take us to the next most important scene in this past life on the count of three. What do you see now?

R: Mom's yelling. I got pregnant. I am 22. Some man from the pub raped me. I thought I was old enough to drink.

L: Do you recognize his soul essence as anyone you know in Regina's life today?

R: He is my recent boyfriend. A couple of months ago we broke up. His name is Chris. The man in the pub is married. He says to give the baby up for adoption. I wanted to show everyone that I was grown up. My father has gone to find the man. Next I see that I am bleeding. The time is close for the baby to be born. Mom tells me to lie down. She gets the doctor and Mrs. O'Reilly. She is old now. She says breathe or I will lose the baby. She gives me a bitter tonic to relax. The doctor says push. The baby comes out. She is so little. I name her Annabelle.

L: Do you recognize Annabelle as anyone you know in your present life?

R: No, I do not know her. I am so excited that she's okay. But I know that I must start a home of my own. I make a home in the forest. Tommy cuts down logs and leave the dog for protection. Men are all drunks, I have decided.

L: Please move us to the next most important scene in this past life. What is happening now?

R: I am standing on the beach. I am 34 years old. I am with a man who has bright blue eyes. His name is John. He helped raise Annabelle. I do not recognize him as anyone I know today. He is trying to convince me to get on a boat to go to America. This is to meet his family. We go. We settle into a dry climate. I feel out of place. John and his dad look for land to build a house. John wants to be a rancher. We get the house and I have four more children in our new home in America.

L: Let's move onto the next scene in this past life where an important event is happening.

R: I am on the porch and the sun is setting. I am rocking my great grandbaby. I am 75 years old. John is 80. We were healthy. I picked all the herbs and learned how to use them. John is on the roof. He falls off the roof. He won't wake up. It kills him. I see the funeral.

L: Let's move to the last day of your life in this past life on three. Where are you?

R: Annabelle is next to me. She's taking care of me. Scott, my little brother, is there.

L: When you are ready, let your soul slowly slip away from Jezebel's body. You will not feel any pain. And now you are drifting off into an upper realm of an all-knowing spiritual power. Here is where you will meet your soul group and your spirit guides. I want you to ask that your spirit guides come through now and help us to understand the life you were just shown.

R: Gaycia. He is my master guide. He is happy and strong. He is very big. He looks like a Greek. He reminds me of Athena. Then I see a guide who looks like a fox and he wants to be called "Fox." I also see a bear. They are hiding behind Talia. Talia is a fairy. She has red hair.

She has a long petal dress on. She is very small. She can sit on my hand. She feels motherly. She knows I have had problems. I have lost people that are close to me in this life. She says that I am not alone. She is always there with me.

R: I grew up in the forest. I am part of the trees. I am an elemental. That is why I was so naïve in that past life. I am still new at this human stuff. I have lived only fifty lives as a human. Most of my lives have been as an elemental. I have been an elemental much longer than I have been human. I am here to learn about humans. I am here to learn why they are spreading over the land.

L: Why were you shown this life?

R: My guides say that with every pain comes happiness. The happiness of having children was at the cost of my being raped and afraid of drunk men of my town. We all encounter the same problems, and we can overcome them, my guides say.

L: Will you ask your guides if you will have a meaningful relationship in this present life?

R: Yes, they say. He will be someone like your John from the Ireland and America life. But I have to wait. It is not the soul of John, but he has kind eyes like John. I am going to meet him in the next couple of years. My spirit guides ask that I not be bitter about mankind. They say that much has to change with humans. We are selfish and think only of ourselves. My guides say that there will be magic again. My guides say that there will be fairies and elementals in future generations. This is a time of rejoicing. The disasters only bring us together.

In reading Regina's past life, you recognized that she was extremely innocent and naïve for her age even in the 1600s. Then you later understand why. She had had only 50 lifetimes as a human. If we are to believe that most of us have had hundreds and hundreds of lives on planet Earth as it matured to today's high vibrational level, then you can appreciate Jezebel's innocence at having experienced only a few lives at that time as a human, not an elemental.

The message from these sessions is that we humans and the elementals must work together to save our dear planet Earth, not oppose each other.

CHAPTER TEN
LIGHT BEINGS AS HUMAN SOULS

For those who believe,
no words are necessary.
For those who do not believe,
no words are possible.
Saint Ignatius of Loyola[13]

The feeling that you don't belong on Earth is a common theme in past life regression work. Some clients just "know" they are from some other planet or galaxy. Others have fallen into depression and/or have headaches or throat problems that cannot be cured. When I meet these particular clients, they have typically already exhausted traditional medicine remedies and found that nothing relieved their pain. Still other clients feel very alone and confused about their lives. They have become depressed with their day-to-day existence. As a last resort, these clients are hoping that past life regression work can shed some understanding on why they suffer so.

Through past life regression therapy, my clients and I have discovered that many souls are light beings. Many souls are light beings from other homes beyond Earth. These

---

[13] Saint Ignatius of Loyola and Anthony Mottola (Jan. 7, 1964), *Spiritual Exercises of Saint Ignatius* (New York, NY: Doubleday div. of Bantam Doubleday Dell Publishing Group Inc., 1964), 2.

clients have come with jobs to do to help planet Earth. Kristi Aronson called me for a past life regression after attending a group session. She said I know I am an older soul, but I want to know where I came from and why I feel so different and alone." As we began the regression, Kristi blurted out quickly many, many statements. Kristi connected with her higher soul self directly. With the guidance of her spirit guides, Kristi was able to understand her mission on earth. She had been holding these feelings in for so long, she didn't hesitate to speak her message to me.

K: (Crying) I can't go home! I'm stuck here. I am responsible and I will do my duty.

L: Please describe your surroundings for me.

K: I am floating, it's like being in a womb. I feel enclosed and protected. I just feel other energy around me, not so much the feeling of other souls around me, just energy.

K: I am not anywhere in particular, I am just "being." I am in the 12th Vibration of Lightbody. I am next to the Creative Source. My heart is so much bigger. (Crying) I feel the back of the heart chakra and the heart chakra is so much bigger. It makes me sad because it reminds me of home. I am guided by the Archangels.

L: How do you connect to the Archangels?

K: They support me. There are many others like me working here, too. There are many at my light level. There are hundreds like me. I don't co-mingle with the other dimensions. I can communicate with them, but I am not with them. I would recognize them in human form, but I would not know why they are here. It's where we all come from. I haven't been back. If I had ever gone home, I would not want to come back to Earth.

K: I do go to the 12th Vibration of Lightbody. It's less of a distraction than trying to go home. We don't feel like separate beings there. On this planet, we meet up, but we don't mingle together. But we have full lives on Earth to do what we are supposed to do while we are here.

L: What is your main path or goal while you are here?

K: I screwed up. I didn't do something right. I didn't fix things for the planet. It is something to do with iron. I was to forge it. I see myself pulling it apart and lengthening and spreading it, instead of leaving it in chunks. (Crying) I didn't do it! It was supposed to be done then.

K: That is why I so like Middle Earth. I don't think it matters any more. I'm still trying to fix what I did wrong. I am still trying to correct my mistake and be perfect. I am still feeling like I hate myself. I am doing some things for the good of Earth. I am helping people. I am changing things.

L: How are you helping other people?

K: I am raising energy. I am pulling the plug on negativity. The duality, the dark and the light, is being changed by my relationships. By having relationships one-on-one, I am changing their opinions. I change things when I let go of things. It breaks the energy and makes it release.

I put a hole in some idea another has, and it weakens it for others.

K: If I could let go of my rejection issues, it makes it easier for others to let go. That ball of energy that I have propels people to shift. This is my last lifetime. I was in energy only, (not in body), when I came back to Middle Earth.

K: I BLEW IT UP! I made a mistake! It was a crystal. I was using it as energy to work with the iron. I blew up the crystal and then we couldn't do what we needed to do. It was in Lemuria. I was an engineer working with the crystal. OH NO, OH NO! The crystal blew. It killed us all. Twenty-five people were killed. I was trying to be really careful. I was trying to get it to do something the crystal couldn't do. I was just trying to make it adapt to do something for a reason. Now I see that we needed to do it to survive. We tried to adapt it. It was more for survival of a small group. We starved to death. We did not die from the explosion. A small group was left. These survivors of Lemuria moved to the edge of Mt. Shasta. We were trying to use the crystal as a heat source. We wanted to heat the iron to make a tool to kill animals to eat and survive.

Kristi came out of the regression exhausted but relieved to let go of the anger and depression. She now understood why she had these depressive feelings. And she clearly was relieved that this was to be her last human life. She was ready to go home, her true home. Many spiritual postings have been written about the higher vibrations. Most speak of the 12th Vibration of Lightbody as being the level where Archangels reside and the level directly below the source of creation.

In Tashira Tachi-Ren's book, *What is Lightbody?*, she states that:

> "Your Lightbody is a gridwork of light and sacred geometry that brings together your physical, emotional, mental, and spiritual being. This body radiates light energy and electromagnetically links your multidimensional self with the infinite universe. It connects you to your encoded data through high electrical currents that assist you in translating and manifesting your hidden talents and soul purpose. As you activate, build and integrate your Lightbody, you reorganize your molecular structure, allowing your body to be less dense and more free to express itself with the source of the universe."

> "The sacred geometry of the Lightbody is also called the 'Merkaba.' This is both an Egyptian and Hebrew word for the spinning field of light energy and information that radiates from the human body as the star tetrahedron, also known as the Star of David. The Merkaba is a geometrically precise field that is formed from the pattern of the first eight veils of the fertilized ovum or zygote. The location of these eight cells is in the geometrical center of the human body in the base or root chakra. The eight cells also provide the center point for all of the energy fields and grids that surround the body. Thus, the Merkaba field is the matrix of creation. Stated another way, it is the blueprint from

which your physical and subtle bodies are
formed and from which your life's journey
and soul purpose is made manifest."[14]

Kristi Aronson was very clear in her role on earth once she connected to her higher self. Along with her spirit guides, her higher self reminded her that she resided in the 12th Vibration of Lightbody. According to Archangel Ariel who is channeled in the book, "*What is Lightbody,*" the 12th vibration is where the archangels reside and it's the closest vibration to the I AM or the Creator. Kristi at last had her answers to where she had come from. She came from an entirely different realm. No wonder she felt out of place on Earth. Her true home vibration was of a higher realm called the 12th Vibration where archangels reside in spirit form and she is here to help save our planet from destruction by humans.

The next client pondering these lonely feelings was Mary Carillo, whom I met in October of 2011 in Denver. Her desire for a past life regression was to find out where she had come from. She wanted to know what other universe her soul spirit had come from. She knew it was not originally planet Earth.

In answering her questions, her higher soul self and her spirit guides told her where she had most recently come from before she made the transition to her life on Earth.

L: Please tell me the first thing you feel and see.

M: I see stars. I see outer space. I feel I am a white ethereal
       light soaring past the stars. I can see the planets. I am

---

[14] Tashira Tachi-Ren, *What is Lightbody?* (Lithia, Springs:
World Tree Press, 1999), Page 71.

not looking at our solar system. I am now on a blue planet. It's cloudy. I am moving through the fog. The ground is like red dirt. There are veins. Beings are a twisting form of glowy light with the veins as their core. The core is blue light and iridescent. The beings have a head shaped like humans but they do not have a nose, eyes or a mouth. They are just pulsing light with these veins in them. The planet is called "Gareon." It is in a far-away galaxy. The trees are twisted with lights running through the same veins on them. Underneath the trees is a portal. I drop through the portal and I am floating down. It looks like the sky inside the blue planet. This is where we live. There is light here, no fog. The white fog is only on the surface of the planet.

M: Everything is made up of this twisted, pulsating light with veins in it. The trees are the same. The structures are similar to what you would see in Atlantis. There are pointy crystal-like buildings everywhere. But even the buildings have the twisty veins pulsating with light through them as well. There are more beings like me. We all sort of glide over the surface. This is the core of the planet. This is where we come from. We are all connected. In one of the structures is our core center. We go back to this core to heal. We don't have human emotions. "Lithicus" is our nation. My name is Aureol. They are telling me that I am staying on Earth for now. "Martruis" is my master guide. He is from another realm. Other beings are here, but not many. They fly or float around. We are all part of a cycle. We have to keep moving. We are eternal.

M: We come into other forms such as humans as a cycle. I had to come. I was to represent Earth and to take care of it. I am a healer. I heal with my hands that have light through them. I am supposed to heal with my hands as well as the light. I am here, but I also help the others. I am a caretaker to them on our planet, Gareon. I am to heal on Earth and create a movement. I am helping Earth to shift. I work on environmental change on many levels. I have to reach people on different levels. If it is necessary, we will work on all levels such as economic, social and environmental. There are less than ten of us on Earth. My guides are ascended beings of light. They are older and more advanced. They are the ones who teach me everything. They look like me. They think themselves here. They would be invisible to humans.

M: I do struggle with the human body. As I age, I will be better able to handle the differences. We are very adaptable. We turn the switch off and on. The body and I are a team. She's doing great. I have been many other places. It's a very big part of my past because we live forever. We soar to get here. The way we get here to the realm of humans is that we "move" energy. There is no portal, but we just enter the womb. I am independent. I have this part of the planet that I work within. Others, like me, work with other sections of Earth.

Mary is an advanced being that has been sent to Earth at this time of its shift to help mankind move forward into a higher realm. She is here to help make this transition peaceful and loving by holding the light wherever she goes. Her higher soul self can control her very strong light energy and use it wherever there is stuck, dark energy that needs to be shifted to help all of mankind transcend to the 5th dimension.

Joanne Petrelli came to me very frustrated. She had picked up an old flyer of one of my sessions on past life regression work from Buena Vista, Colorado, from 2009. She sounded alarmed over the phone as she set up an appointment to see me for a regression. She is a teacher and suddenly the children were really starting to upset her. This had never happened to her before. She told her husband it must be the new move to Buena Vista, CO. Then she had had many physical ailments to do with her throat and thyroid. I was hoping that we could get to the reason for her ailments through her subconscious mind.

Joanne is a client who was blocking her human self from awakening to her mission as a light being while she was here on earth. I believe that is why her physical ailments were getting worse. She needed to speak truth and use her light power. As the regressions unfold, it's clear that the advanced being of Joanne wants to tell her of her abilities and skills. Joanne saw two very quick lives pertaining to her question of why she held onto so much anger and why could she not get rid of her throat and thyroid problems. I was hoping Joanne would allow more to come through for her.

J: I am outside, and there is yellow grass all around me.

L: Please describe what you look like and what you are wearing.

J: I have on black shoes, tights and a red plaid dress. I have short dark hair and it's the 1950s.

L: What is your name?

J: My name is Micha and I am 3 or 4 years old. I am chasing the dog and I see that my dad comes and picks it up and takes it inside.

L: Do you recognize your parents as anyone you know in your current life as Joanne?

J: Yes, my mother is my mother in my present life and my father is my grandfather in my present life. Next I see that I am laughing but also choking at the same time. My mother has just thrown something at me and it hits me. It is a plate. I fall down and then I get up and sit down. My throat hurts. She has done this, along with my dad, before. It's because I keep talking. They want me to be quiet.

L: Let's please move to the next most important scene in this past life we are experiencing on the count of three. One, two, three...

J: I am in a car and I am driving. I am a young person. I am on a road near the water. I am happy as I drive along the coast. I am in my 20s. I work with flowers and go to school. My parents are still alive. I am underwater! I was trying to put music in to listen to and my right rear tire skidded off the road and I went down into the water. The car went down backward and it falls on top of me. It was a convertible. I feel like I am struggling to get out. I was hit on the head and soon I became unconscious. My soul leaves me before I die. I fell off the right side of the cliff. The road was high on the cliff. I went through the guard rail and I struggled as I went down, but I knew that I was dying.

L: We are now going to float up above the scene and move up into the clouds. As you drift, you see a beautiful meadow just up ahead. There are beautiful wild flowers blowing in the wind and grasses gently swaying. You slowly drift down to the meadow and smell the grass, and feel the wind in your face. Now, as you are observing the meadow, I am going to ask some very simple questions.

L: Is it day or night and are you inside a structure or outside?

J: It is nighttime. I am outside and I see a path. I see lights below like a village. I am barefooted with bare legs. I have a long shirt on. I am dirty. I have short hair.

L: Could you tell me about yourself?

J: I am a boy about 12 or 13. My name is Unte. I am Asian. It is Thailand or Tibet. It is the 1700s. I am eating. I am eating rice out of a wooden bowl. Everyone knows me. I live on the streets. I am mentally disabled. My family died of some disease. I am always joking around. The town likes me. Oh no, they stab me! I threw rice at someone and they stabbed me. It's a visitor. He is a man and he is white.

L: Do you recognize his soul essence as anyone in your present life today?

J: Yes, my husband Chris. The man has a dagger. I am slow. "You're a nuisance," he says. He is having a meeting. He is a drug dealer. He is trying to make a deal. I mess it up and I didn't know it when I threw the rice. I see his eyes. He has piercing blue eyes. I realize he is coming at me. I can see the blade in front of my face. He sticks it in my throat. He jabs it in my throat. There is a lot of blood. I cough. People come to help me. Everyone tries to help. He just walks away. They yell at him, but they are afraid of him. That life I lived like an animal outside. People gave me food to keep me alive.

L: You will now float above that life and will feel no pain
      as you rise to a higher vibration. This vibrational space
      is where your spirit guides reside. Please, on the count
      of three, ask your guides to come through and tell you
      more about the past lives you just experienced.

J: My master guide is a unicorn, and his name is Dante. He
      is strong, happy, noble and laughing. Next, I see Crow.
      Crow is kind of gruff. He is old and he seems wise, stern,
      inpatient. I see a third entity as pure purple and green.
      It is loving and watching. It is my higher self.

L: What can your spirit guides tell us about the past lives
      in relation to your question about your throat?

J: You need to live more from your heart, they say. They
      say be yourself.

J: Dante says that the way to help the thyroid is to connect
      to the "I AM" and if you move from the school you
      are working in, it will help, he says. He says that if I
      continue on with my therapy with the doctors, it will
      help within the year. He says that acupuncture will also
      help. I need to relax more.

J: Now he is telling me more. I am running out of time.
      I need to be myself. That means more than I can
      understand. He is telling me I am to do what I came to
      do. Be myself and use my skills. I came from the stars
      and I need to be using the energy that I brought with
      me. I am to use the light stream that I brought with me.
      How can I activate the light stream? It will attract things
      to me, if I will use it. I am afraid to attract attention.
      They say I will only attract the light. I am seeing things,
      they say. The stars I see are to remind me that I am full

of energy. When Crow gets inside of me, my arms will absorb the energy and I will send it out my fingers.

J: They say that I am to be teaching the children something to do with their brains. I am to teach them to bring this energy to their brains and their hearts, just like I can. Then later they will transmute the light through their bodies to others. This is to help raise the vibration of all humankind.

As Joanne came back into the room, she was still very upset. She did not want this role on earth. Here is a light being who does not understand her role even after being told by her guides why she is here. She has no interest in finding out. A week later, I emailed Joanne and called her to see what she had processed from our session. She did feel better about the sore throat and thyroid problems she had been having, and felt there was hope in her treatment. She did understand why her higher self and her spirit guides showed her two important lives that left her very sensitive to issues with her throat, but she still failed to understand her contribution as a light being to help others. Probably the anger and occasional migraines were still being caused by her strong denial to her soul self that she was here on Earth at this time to use her energy to transmute light to others.

Joanne's last comment before she left our session was "I feel so all alone here." Even though she had earlier identified her brother as also being from her home planet, she felt there were no other souls supporting her in her mission. Maybe that is why she had not fully stepped into her soul's path.

The following case of James Saloman also shows a life of a light being on planet Earth, but James Saloman's headaches were much more than just physical ailments that brought him to me. I met James' mother at a metaphysical book store in Denver at an event where she was one of the facilitators at the store. Her son, James, who was 21, came to me later for an intuitive reading. Then several months later he called me for help. He had been suffering from severe headaches that had started to affect his ability to work. His mother had told him of my past life regression work, and he was hoping that a session with me would hold the key to his suffering.

His questions for his regression session were many. He wanted to know why he had a sharp, stabbing pain in his head. He said his head had been throbbing for over two years with no relief. He was sleepy all the time. He stated that he drank no caffeine, hoping to help the pain go away.

The first scene that James could describe for me was in a cave.

J: I am inside a closed-in area. I can sense water, a stream. It feels like I am in a cave. I am trying to get a candle to see. The walls look like embedded rock.

L: Would you please describe what you are wearing.

J: I have on metal shoes. I have metal on my legs, and metal on my chest. It's some kind of armor. I have a poncho on over it. It's steel, and it looks like a knight's armor.

L: What is the year and what part of the country are you in?

J: It's 1704 and I am in Turkey.

L: What is your name?

J: My name is Somay. I am holding up my sword. I am by myself and I am scared. I am trying to get out. It starts to get cold. I don't want to get wet from the water in the cave. I keep trying to find a way out. Finally I build a fire. I take my armor off. But the shield on my face won't come off. I get the fire going. I find rocks and sticks to try to get the helmet off.

J: Now I see an opening. It's daylight and I get out. The armor is so tight on my skin that it almost sticks to my skin. I can't explain the relationship of the metal to my skin. It's too difficult to explain. I am trying to stop the fear. I don't know how I got to this place.

J: Now I see that a meteor came. I was on that meteor and it shot me to this planet. I found myself falling from the meteor through space into this atmosphere and to this planet.

L: Where are you from, Somay?

J: "Honahot-he-chey." It's the beginning from where we all come. The sun is red. I am a traveling being. I am not from any one planet. I am trying to see the world. I am trying to understand evil. It's a new feeling. I feel the hate on this planet. It kills me. It feels like a disease. These feelings are all very new to me. That is why I keep my helmet on. I am trying to bring the light here. But I can't bring the light here because of the evil. I am trying so hard. But I can't because of the evil here. I pray to the Creator, the Oneness. I tell of the evil here. But I can't explain how I do this. I am from the beginning of creation.

J: I am getting scared, now. I eat by drinking water and taking in light. I can subsist on the light.

L: I want us to move to the next important scene in this past life you are experiencing on the count of three. One, two, three.

J: I see lava. I see hot lava. I am trying to get to the water. I reach the water. The lava is burning me. It's hurting my head. I am in the ocean. It's burning me, as I try to cool the helmet. Now I see land. The land now looks different than it had. I stay. I stay 54,000 years in the water. I still have my armor on. I see the moon. I want to die. I want to cry. I want to bring the light and the love. The time is too soon to bring the light. There are two parts of me. One part of me is in James, and the other is in Somay. Somay is in the darkness. It's very hard to describe. I have stayed in the darkness all this time. Somay is in the ocean under a rock formation. I (Somay) am still not able to bring the light and love to the planet. Everything's going to die.

L: James, I want you to ask your spirit guides to come in now and help us understand Somay and this past life on the count of three. One, two, three.

J: What is causing my headaches? My guides say it's the helmet. It's hurting Somay, so it is also hurting James. Somay can't take it off.

L: Can he help relieve James' pain? Can he lift the helmet off James' head?

J: My spirit guides say it time for Somay to go with them. Sometimes we come for him. Somay says he fights to stay here to help. There is going to be a lot of death on the planet. Somay's guides say they are afraid he will die if he stays here... How soon will you come for him?

They say in 2014. In a meteor, they will come to get him.

J: They say it is not my decision to stay or go.

L: Can they take away the pain James is suffering now?

J: They say they can help me with the pain. This is why I see the beings. The beings have wanted to talk to me. Somay wants to live a human life through me. They say they are trying to send Somay love and light. This is why he has been here so long. He is waiting to bring love and light to the planet when it needs it most. The guides say I can communicate with them. They are coming for Somay. It's an ancient language that they speak, and I can't understand. They are telling me, "to the man that comes." Please speak English... Somay tells me he knows that I am mad. I was trying to be a warrior, but I can't with the headaches. Somay is telling me he wants to take off the helmet to help me with my pain. Somay says the Earth is sick because of the evil. Somay says that this has happened before. He is a guardian. He is waiting. He has a staff. He controls the light. That is his job to be here. He says he will help take the helmet off so James' pain will stop.

James was extremely tired when the session ended. He did feel some of the pressure in his head had been relieved. This session was very confusing to understand, but I believe that Somay is a being of light who came thousands of years ago and made his home in the ocean, waiting for the time to bring light and love to planet Earth. This light being, Somay, was so devastated by the pain and hatred on the planet that he himself suffered because of it. He had entered part of his spirit into James to be a being on earth to try to adjust to being here. But the pain was just too great. I believe his fellow light beings will be coming for him soon. I do believe James will be left to live his life without the pain and will accomplish his own path separate from Somay. In the meantime, it's comforting to know we are not fighting the darkness alone. There are many unseen advanced light beings here now to help us.

I believe the advanced beings we are waiting for to help us in our time of need to save humans and our beloved planet from destruction are not coming in ships or materializing on earth in a last-minute effort to save us. I believe they have been here all along, as part of our civilization. The Hopi Nation knows this and sent this letter around the world recently to have us wake up to the idea that our saviors are here and they are US.

The Hopi Elders Speak
The Elders, Oraibi, Arizona, Hopi Nation
March 28, 2011

"We Are the Ones We've Been Waiting For"

You have been telling the people that this
is the Eleventh Hour.

Now you must go back and tell the people
that this is The Hour.

And there are things to be considered:

Where are you living?

What are you doing?

What are your relationships?

Are you in right relation?

Where is your water?

Know your garden.

It is time to speak your Truth.

Create your community. Be good to each other. And do not look outside yourself for the leader. This could be a good time!

There is a river flowing now very fast. It is so great and swift that there are those who will be afraid. They will try to hold on to the shore. They will feel they are being torn apart, and they will suffer greatly.

Know the river has its destination. The elders say we must let go of the shore, push off into the middle of the river, keep our eyes open, and our heads above the water.

See who is in there with you and celebrate.

At this time in history, we are to take nothing personally. Least of all, ourselves.

For the moment that we do, our spiritual growth and journey comes to a halt.

The time of the lone wolf is over. Gather yourselves!

Banish the word struggle from your attitude and your vocabulary.

All that we do now must be done in a sacred manner and in celebration.

We Are the Ones We've Been Waiting For. [15]

---

[15] *We Are The Ones We Have Been Waiting For, The Hopi Elders Speak,* Attributed to an unnamed Hopi Elder, Hopi Nation, Oraibi, Arizona

CHAPTER ELEVEN
SEXUAL ABUSE IN PRESENT AND PAST LIVES

Up to this chapter, sexual abuse experienced in past, or present lives, has only been discussed in this book in Chapter Eight, with Janine's case of panic attacks. The following cases deal directly with trauma that clients have dealt with throughout their lives concerning sexual abuse they experienced. They put these traumatic episodes out of their memory in the present life. Sometimes the original trauma can be discovered from previous lives and clients find it repeated in their present life. Research has shown that our body's cells have memory of our trauma from the past. When the soul enters our present body it brings all the feelings from these relationships into the new body to attempt to overcome them in this lifetime.

Sarah Millman is a successful business owner in her early 60s from Colorado Springs whom I met in June of 2012. She had had physical ailments for years that affected her thyroid. She had aches and pains throughout her body. She also complained of stomach aches that resembled the pain from stomach ulcers. She was being treated by a naturopathic doctor as well as an internal medicine doctor. But her ailments never seemed to lessen. I suggested that a past life regression might reveal clues to her health problems.

After Sarah easily relaxed into a light trance, she came upon a girl of 15 in Minnesota.

S: I see myself doing laundry in my family's home. I am not married. My mother's name is Jenny. I have siblings who are John, Brenda, Melissa, and Linda. Then I see that Dad comes home.

L: Let's now move to the next most important scene in your life in Minnesota on the count of three. One, two, and three.

S: I am in a field and there are flowers and trees. I am still a teenager. I am going down the road. I see a white house. I walk in the door and my Aunt Dora is inside. She brings out cookies and we talk.

L: If there is not anything else we should see in this scene, let's now move to the next most important scene in your life in Minnesota on the count of three. One, two, and three.

S: I am working at the local furniture store. I only work there part time. I am still only 16 years old. The owner is Mr. Strauss. He is real bossy and he is Jewish. The manager is a man and to do his job, he moves very fast over the floor where the furniture is displayed. I work the cash register. All the people that work on the sales floor are Jewish and they are very "cutthroat" to each other to make their individual sales. I just answer the phone and ring up the sales. At the store, I see that a customer comes in to put the moves on me. His name is Hugh and he is 40 years old.

Sarah had already told me that she was from Minnesota and had grown up there. With that information, I deduced that this was her present life as a young girl. Yet, I could feel these scenes unfolding for her like a lost part of her past that she had pushed so far down in her psyche that she was only able to retrieve them through this hypnotherapy light trance. I continued on with the session to see what unfolded.

S: Hugh takes me to the house of one of my friends, who dates an older man. I see that Hugh fondles me, but does not have intercourse with me. I am happy that it's not scary. It's my first time to do any of this. He takes me to my car. Shortly afterward he moves to Florida...

S: There is another man much like Hugh. He works at another furniture store that I get transferred to. He is also about 40 years old. I am still 16. He wants me to take care of him. I am sucking his dick. He finally moves away from town.

S: Next, I see that I have a physical problem. I go to the doctor to see what is wrong with me. I went without my mother. I am bleeding from the rectum. I go to the doctor to do the physical exam and I am the last appointment and he fondles me during the exam. He sends the nurse home who assists him. Next, he tells me that he will show me how to have an orgasm. I am naïve and I think it's the thing to do. I go to my car afterward. I go home then and do not tell anyone.

S: I wonder if the doctor ever gets picked up as a sexual offender in his practice. My medical problem was a fissure. It is a hole between the uterus and the intestines. I am 17 now. I finally move away to go to college. In college, in about a year, I meet my husband Don. We are still married today.

L: Would you tell me a little more about your life as you left for college?

S: My parents are very conservative and they question my getting married at such a young age. I am only 19. Don uses marijuana and they find my birth control. Dad brings Don in for a talk and Don tells my dad that he plans on marrying me. Dad becomes okay after Don explains how he feels about me. We move to Colorado after graduating from college.

L: Let's ask your spirit guides to come through to help us more with the scenes they showed you.

S: I see that my master guide is Violet. All she is showing me is the scenes I just relayed to you.

After Sarah sat up and she recovered from her induction, we discussed the scenes. I told Sarah, "Rather than go to a past life, your higher self and your spirit guides showed you what is causing all the pain you are experiencing right now in your body. To answer your question about why you cannot heal yourself, the scenes were shown to you to help you remember that you were sexually abused for a period of several years when you were 16 to 18 years old by several men, including a man you trusted. Your family doctor raped you. The older men abused you and later had sex with you, and you thought you had to do it. They were very pushy and you did not know how to tell them no. You didn't have feelings for these older men. You were so young and innocent. They took advantage of you because they could. Then they moved away and you didn't have to tell anyone what happened. But you held it in all these years. You didn't tell your mother, or your aunt." Sarah told me later, she had never told anyone what happened. Not even her girlfriends. Instead, she poured herself into her business and became a workaholic to try to forget the pain. She had a loveless marriage and never had wanted children.

I recommended a therapist for Sarah to go to for further release of the pain and heartache she was carrying around with her, all these years later. She knew when I asked her about her stomach pains, that it was because of all the anger she was holding onto for these men that abused her.

Marilyn Atkinson is the owner of her own in-home business in the Brighton, Colorado, area. She found one of my flyers from the book store in Colorado Springs and gave me a call for a past life regression. Marilyn was extremely attractive and looked much younger than her age of 43. She was married to a great partner who helped her in her business, along with his own massage practice. They had two children, plus her husband had a grown daughter from a previous marriage. When we talked on the phone before our meeting, Marilyn seemed very concerned that she was not doing something in her life that she was called to do. But she was not clear at all what that could be. She had been dealing with her attractiveness to men as a liability all her life, and wondered why she felt this way.

When we were talking before beginning the session, Marilyn also related to me that she felt a special bond with her husband's assistant that did not seem natural. It was almost like a sexual attraction. She felt very uncomfortable about this feeling when she was around Brian. She was in her early 40s and he was 19. She also stated that she really loved her husband, and wondered why she would have this strange feeling for his assistant.

M: I feel I am in a room. I see light in the left part of the room. The light is above me. Now I see pictures on the wall, and I feel something behind me. It is a chandelier. There is an expensive table, a dining table, the expensive chandelier hangs over. I see an elaborate china cabinet.

L: Let's take a look at you. What are you wearing, starting with your shoes?

M: I have on boots, and I am wearing a skirt with a petticoat underneath. I have on a cinched cummerbund dress with short sleeves. The dress is low cut.

L: Pretend that you put a mirror in front of your face and tell me any details about your face and hair.

M: I have long dark hair and I look to be in my twenties.

L: What is your name and where do you feel you are?

M: My name is Jenny and I am in England.

L: What year is it? What is the first number that pops into your head?

M: It's 1841. I am only visiting in this house. I am a servant here. There is an employer. It is a man, and his name is Frederick. I feel like he expects me to be available for sex. It is required of me. It's part of my job there. His wife Jennifer knows we are having sex, but prefers to do nothing about it. I see myself start to do the chores of the house.

L: Let's now move to the next most important scene in this past life of Jenny's on the count of three. One, two, and three.

M: I see children playing. They are not mine, but I have adopted them or am taking care of them. I am going to protect them. I am slowly letting go of the dress look, and moving into a more casual caretaker attire. We are all on a cobblestone road and they are playing and are happy. We gather around and they tell me of their happy and sad moments of the day. I am their teacher. So now I see hundreds of them. I am being shown that all my adult life in this life, I was a teacher for many, many children. They brought their hopes and their dreams to me.

L: Do you recognize any of their soul essences as anyone you know in today's life as Marilyn?

M: Some feel familiar, but I do not see any names I recognize in my life today. Now I see that it's the end of the day, and I go home. I am alone. I am still in my 20s.

L: Are your parents still alive?

M: My parents have died. They died tragically. They were killed. Someone didn't like them and they killed them. My parents didn't do anything wrong. They might have been a different kind of couple and they were persecuted for that.

L: Do you recognize the soul essence of your parents as anyone you know in your life as Marilyn?

M: Yes, my mother is Laura, my mother today. I do not recognize my father in that life.

L: Let's move to the next most important scene in Jenny's life on the count of three.

M: I am much older now. I am in my 80s. I am walking to town to get bread. I have no family. I still live in the same town. Everyone likes me, but I prefer to be alone. I feel good about my life, but there is something that holds me back from living fully.

L: Let's move to the last day of this past life of Jenny as I count from one to three, and on three you will be in the last day of your life as Jenny.

M: I am in a bed. I am alone and I am across from a cross that has Jesus on it. I wish that I had had the courage to live more fully in this life.

L: When you are ready, just let your soul slowly slip away from Jenny. You will feel no pain. And now as your soul self is rising above the final scene of Jenny, is there anything you would like to do before you leave?

M: I would like to say goodbye to all the kids. I love all of you. They are answering back to me in feelings that they love me, too.

L: Now you will be floating up to a higher realm of an all-loving spiritual power. And I would like for you to now ask that your spirit guides join us when I count to three. They will help you understand why your higher soul self and your spirit guides showed you this very important past life to help answer your questions.

M: I see Joseph. He is kind, not overbearing. He probes me for my questions. Next I feel Mary. She is a similar personality to Joseph. She is wearing a blue robe. She is in her 30s. Directly out in front of me I see the Archangel Gabriel.

L: Could you ask one more question about Jenny's life. What year did she die?

M: 1912. It was barbaric the way my parents were killed. They were stoned to death. People were afraid of them.

They were both very psychic, and just connected to God. They had many gifts in clairvoyance. People feared them. I was 8 years old when they died. It is interesting that in my current life, my father died when I was 9. My spirit guides all say that I am also highly gifted now, but I am afraid to let it out because my parents were killed for it in Jenny's life. That's who I am, they are telling me. The guides are very calm about it. They ask me if I want to use my skills. I am afraid I will scare people as my parents did in that past life. Then they were killed because the people were afraid. My spirit guides say just approach it in your everyday life as a part of who you are. Just use your skills in all that you do with others.

L: Please ask your guides about your relationship with your husband's assistant, Brian.

M: They say he really admires me and loves me. I ask them if he will grow out of this attraction for me as he matures. They say right now it's confusing for him. The way he feels.

L: Please ask your spirit guides if you have had a previous life with the soul of Brian.

M: It's more like he has wanted a life with me, but has never had one with me. The spirit guides are telling me that I should just let him develop his life and I should be very kind to him along the way. They say don't avoid him, just be mature when I am with him and do not play into any of his emotions.

M: Sometimes there is a part of me that does things to play into men's attraction for me. But part of me knows that

I better not act on my feelings, as well. I feel I have been sexually abused when I was very young. This previous life seems that I was also sexually used. I am aware that it doesn't create any good thoughts to think that it's my job to make men feel good. (As she was made to do in Jenny's life as the servant who had to perform sexually for her employer.) My guides are telling me I don't have to give it away to men. They need to earn it. Brian might be testing me on this. His being in my life is not a coincidence. We will both learn from our relationship.

L: You need to ask your spirit guides to help you let these feelings go of pleasing men. Ask them to help you set boundaries for yourself. Ask for their help at all times.

M: I feel this sexual abuse as a young child for me was from my mother. The guides are showing me that my mother abused me sexually when I was three. She fondled me.

L: Why did she do this to you?

M: The guides say she was curious. I can't forgive her. She meant to hurt me. Her mother did the same thing to her. My mother was acting out from the pain she had felt.

L: How long did the abuse continue?

M: 5 or 6 years.

As we brought the session to a close, I suggested to Marilyn specific actions to follow in the future to help her release the pain she was carrying around from her mother's abuse. She also left the session much lighter, she said, and less burdened for seeing the past life where she had held so much in. Jenny was afraid to give love to anyone but the innocent children in that life because she had seen her parents killed for being themselves. Since she also had those same attributes, she hid her true self from everyone in her life as Jenny.

Then once again, she had suffered sexual abuse from her mother in this life, and it had made her withdraw into her shell once again. Even though she was happily married, the only arena where she felt safe was her in-home business, when she was dealing with innocent children.

Both Sarah and Marilyn uncovered sexual abuse in their present lives that they had suppressed to the point that they could not consciously remember the actual abuse except under trance. Their higher soul selves and their spirit guides knew it was vitally important that they reveal these emotional scenes in their lives to bring them out in the open. Through past life regression, these clients began to identify the past abuse and release the trauma so that they can experience more complete and loving lives today and in the future.

CHAPTER TWELVE
A FAMILY OF LIGHT BEINGS FROM URABITZIA

Priscilla Daniel and all her immediate family are the subjects of this entire chapter. Of all my experiences with clients in past life regression, Priscilla's was the most interesting and detailed of the lives of a light being. It's important to see that light beings travel in groups just as any other soul group does. Souls return over and over again on earth to be with their loved ones in different roles and many may be from more advanced civilizations than earth. I met Priscilla in February, 2012, when she was working part time in a Denver metaphysical book store where I was performing intuitive readings and past life regressions. When you look at Priscilla, you cannot help but notice the light beaming off her entire body. To look at her eyes takes courage because the light that shines through her eyes is unmistakable. I once told her this very thing. People love to be around Priscilla.

She lights up the room as she walks into it. She always has a smile for each and every person. She is the mother of four daughters, a graduate student of computer technology, happily married to her second husband, and was taking a break from computer work when I met her.

Priscilla heard of my past life regression sessions, and signed up for the first event I had with the store after she started to work there. Her questions sounded simple enough. She wanted to know about past lives with her current husband, Mike, and her four daughters. She wanted to know her spirit guides and her purpose in this life. What came through in the past life regression was much more than what she asked for.

Priscilla went into trance easily and we began in an outdoor scene.

P: It is dusk and I am in yellow grass with flowers in it, and it is knee high. I feel very lightheaded. I feel like I am floating.

L: Look down at yourself and tell me what you are wearing.

P: I have on sandals. They are leather and very primitive. I am wearing light, flowing pants. I have on a flowing tunic over my pants.

L: Priscilla, tell me what you look like.

P: I have long dark hair. I have gold in my hair. I am in my 30s. I have gold bands around my arms. I can feel the grass with my hands.

L: Can you tell me your name and what year it is?

P: My name is Amazue. The year is 170 A.D. I am in Egypt. I see myself walking down a path. I see the pebbles by a river. I have been here before. Floating off to my right, I see a guy. He is a mentor to me. His name is Euz. I feel I can telecommunicate with him. He taught me how to do this. He is very old and wise. I continue walking. He comes from a different time and place than Earth. The planet he is from is Urabitzia. Both of us are from this planet, Urabitzia. I still see him floating. I go to the water. It heals me. My home planet was purple. There was a lot of water on my home planet. I see lots of clouds and fog, as well. I see that I would go underwater there. The water was deep blue, but I was in light form when I traveled in the water.

P: Next I see that I am standing. The water has now turned to gold light, and it's energy. It's coming to me from a distance. I can call it to me. I take the flow and I put it in my hands and I run it through my body. Now, I am being shown outer space. I leave this Earth plane and go there all the time. I see others here on my home planet. They are like light forms. There are five or six. They look like stars in the heavens. Our job is to heal the humans. In Egypt, I am trying to teach this to others. I work with another male to do this. He works with herbs and healing. He is not aware that I'm from another planet. I work with the plants. His name is Ethraz. I see artifacts, stones, dry herbs, and salts. We make healing potions. We work with people who have passed. We deal with the preservation of the body after it has passed, the embalming. I also see lots of gold around us.

L: Do you recognize Ethraz's soul essence as anyone you know in your present life today?

P: Yes, he is Mike, my present husband.

L: I want to count to three, and I want you to move to the next most important scene in this past life in Egypt on the count of three. One, two, and three.

P: I am in my home and I am in my 70s now. I see lots of girls. All of them are my granddaughters. All four of my daughters in my present life are part of this group. They are about 7 to 10 years of age. My partner in this life was Ethraz. I have taught a lot in this life. I was telling stories, and touching others. By touching others, I was passing the light onto them. I communicated with children by transferring the light to them. The stream of light can be passed easily. The stream of light lightens and elevates. On my last day of life, I see that I am still in my seventies and I just go back to light when I leave my body. Next, I go back to my home planet. I see my Council of Elders. There are five of them. They are light forms in different colors. My master guide is there also. Now I am trying to decide how I want to stay in the light. How do I want to use my light? I see the stones. Each stone represents a different life. Each one is a different color. I just pick one up. The Elders know about each life.

L: How do you decide to move to the next life with your Elders?

P: I pick up a light purple stone. It fits in the palm of my hand. It is very porous. I'm holding it to my heart. I'm trying to feel it, trying to ground myself. I am trying to connect to it and become one with it. It goes into my chest. It's a form of light energy. I take it into my heart chakra. It radiates super light.

L: Please tell me what you see next.

P: I am in a lodge. There are other people around. I am female and I am my 30s or 40s. My name is Amber.

L: In this second life, tell me what year it feels like and what part of the country you are in.

P: It is 1787 and I am in the United States somewhere in the Midwest. I am married to Merritt.

L: Do you recognize the soul essence of Merritt as anyone you know in your present life?

P: Yes, it's Mike, my husband today.

L: Please tell me what you see next.

P: I have a little son. He is a baby. His name is Rumor. I don't recognize his soul as anyone I know today. This lodge is a church. It's a white man's lodge. I am Native American. Merritt is a white man. He is part Indian and part white. He is very evolved and I am very evolved. I work with herbs. I'm a healer. I am aware that I am from another place. I know that my home is not Earth. Merritt knows this, too. We use the gold light in this life as well. He helps with the relationship between the white man and the Native American.

L: Now that we have been introduced to this past life, please take us to the next most important scene of Amber's past life on the count of three. One, two, and three.

P: We are in a teepee. It is a sweat lodge. People come to the sweat lodge. I have grown children. The girls are all grown, and they are all my girls today. The boy I see now is the soul of Joanie, my daughter today. We are still holding the light. We heal. We work with stones. People come to us for healing, much like Reiki today. We do rituals. We use singing quite a bit. We use our voices to bring the light. My daughters heal with their voices. The whole family comes from the planet, Urabitzia.

L: Let's now move to the last day of your lives on the count of three. One, two, and three.

P: I see that we are in our late 90s. We are side by side, Merritt and I. We are holding hands as we leave in light.

L: Please now ask your spirit guides to come through and talk to us about why you were shown these particular past lives on the count of three. One, two, and three.

P: There is an older man, Michael. He has a long beard and white hair. He has on a flowing robe. He is showing me that he wears a wizard hat like Merlin. Behind him, I see bright yellow. I feel the healing energy of Archangel Raphael. Next I see little fireflies buzzing. They bring help to lighten things. They bring laughter. They get rid of heavy energy.

L: Let's ask your spirit guides about your spiritual path.

P: I'm here to heal others. I use my hands, the light, the herbs, and oils to heal others. I will be working more intensely in the future. I am here to help my girls, to guide them. To help them raise their vibration.

P: I want to know why I chose my parents. The guides say I have known them. They've taught me before. (Priscilla's father is a chiropractor, her mother is a stay-at-home mom). I am supposed to learn how to have them vibrate on a higher level.

L: May we ask your advanced beings about 2012?

P: We are all moving toward a higher vibration, they say. We will be able to telecommunicate in 2012. There will be a shift to the non-physical by many souls on a grand scale in December, 2012.

L: I have been told about wars in the future by other master beings. Master beings told me there could be danger for Earth if Iran and Israel went to war. What do you see about Iran and Israel starting war between themselves in the future?

P: We can prevent any disasters between these two countries. But we should let it happen. The destruction between these two countries is inevitable.   There will be a new 5D Earth (5th dimension). We will shift to a light body by 2050.   This is all the ascension process. We will all be ready for the changes. All our higher soul selves are prepared for this.... Whenever there is actually a nuclear bomb that goes off on Earth, many souls will ascend... There will be two separate Earths created at that time with two different vibrations. The souls vibrating at a higher vibration will go to the other Earth. The souls vibrating at a lower vibration will stay together and may be the creators of the New Earth. I will go to the other planet. Lee will become a higher vibration and stay to be a warrior to create the new 5D earth.

I think it's important to ask these very ascended beings that are coming through as spirit guides some of these pressing questions about the ascension process. We all are uninformed about what will actually happen when the Mayan calendar runs out on December 21, 2012. I only want to pass along the information I am provided, which I hope will enlighten and inform us all.

Priscilla stated that she felt so much lighter after our session. She had had a sense that something was different about her and her family but didn't know what it was. Now, she had a deeper understanding of her and her family's relationship and their role in this very important time in Earth's history.

The next month, Priscilla wanted to explore the deeper sense of her higher soul self and scheduled a between lives regression to investigate further where she was from. Also, she wanted to understand her past. Why did she carry around feelings of abandonment? Her parents had been there for her as a child. They were both still alive and very close to her. What was causing these feelings to resurface for her time and again.

We started the between lives regression by looking at points in Priscilla's life as we regressed back through her childhood. We returned to her soul meeting her human self while still in the womb. She felt both her parents were excited to be having her and they both loved her. I asked when she connected with the fetus in the womb. She stated it was around 3 months into the pregnancy. She felt the body was strong and that she had a lot of good work she came to do. She felt blessed. She felt special and she felt she could accomplish anything in this life.

As we left the womb, we approached Priscilla's most recent previous life and her first scene was outside in rolling hills.

P: It is daytime and I am outside in the bright light. I am in grassy meadows with rolling hills. I see big rocks. It resembles the rocks you would see at Lake Powell in Utah. There is a lot of sandstone around me.

L: Can you tell me what you are wearing?

P: I have on sandals. I have a loose cotton skirt with an oversized cotton tunic top over it.

L: Pretend you put a mirror in front of your face and describe what you look like.

P: I have long dark hair. I am in my 20s. I am in my late 20s.

L: What year does it feel like?

P: It is 1879 and we are in Utah. I am walking in a gully. I
       live nearby. I am enjoying the day. I am walking back to
       my home. It is a log cabin layered with mud in between
       the logs. I feel comfortable and we are protected by a
       tall cove in front of us. I am married to Tom. He is very
       manly. He is in his 40s. My name is Amber and I have
       two boys.

L: Do you see the names of your children?

P: Yes, they are Brian, three years old, and Todd, five years
       old.

L: Do you recognize the soul essence of your husband?

P: Yes, he is my ex-husband, Ken. I feel sad. I feel lonely.
       It's a hard life. I am not happy with him. He is not strong.
       He is weak inside. I feel trapped. It was a dream of his
       to come out to this rugged country to eke out a life. It
       has not worked out. I am disconnecting from my boys.
       The boys are like their father. I can't seem to relate to
       them. We have nothing to eat. We had money, but it ran
       out. I decide to leave. The boys stay with their father.
       Next I see that the home catches on fire. Tom starts the
       fire and kills the boys and himself! I feel guilty, but I
       am relieved. I walk away (Priscilla is crying). I find a
       place to live. I am alone. It is a deserted camp for the
       soldiers. I find a way to survive.

L: Let's now move to the next most important scene in
       Amber's life in this past life on the count of three. One,
       two, and three.

P: I am in my 30s now. I am still in the camp. I live off fishing and picking berries to eat and survive. I am healing from my family dying, but I feel so alone. I am becoming happy because I get energy from the rocks.

L: Let's now move to the next most important scene in Amber's life in this past life.

P: I am still alone. I am in my 70s now. I am happy and it's very peaceful. I didn't want to find other people. I did rituals to heal myself. I played music. I spent time healing myself. I did worship and gave thanks for my life. I now see myself lying down, and feeling it's time. I look very hard and weathered.

L: To help you put closure to this life with Ken, could you please call his soul essence in and say goodbye? What would you say to him? He will answer you.

P: First of all, I call my boys in. They are putting their arms around me. They tell me they are okay. I tell them I love them. Next, I ask Ken to come through and tell me why he lived the life he did. He says that that life was more for him to learn, than for me. He wants to thank me for showing him how he doesn't want to live again. He says he knows he has a lot to learn. He was confused when he took his life and the boys' lives. The boys had a lot of love for him. All three were caught in that grey energy. I had so much that was stifled. I felt so stagnant. They were energy suckers...

P: Now I suddenly see my soul moving away from Earth. I see bright vivid colors. There is a dark, dark purple. I am in the stars and the atmosphere is purple. I am floating. There are beings around me. I am traveling way out there. I see a planet with light. I sense my guides. I now see these little goldish-white lights buzzing around me. I know that they are Mike and my daughters. They are like orbs. He is the biggest orb. I can see his face in the orb. Now I can see my spirit guides. They are in flowing, white robes, and my master guide Michael has white hair. They are calling me back. I see a light blue color; it is my brother... I see about 20 other lights. It's my soul group. I see Tom and Kirk (Priscilla's siblings), and they are yellow and blue lights, and I see orange peach colors for my parents. They are together...

P: My spirit guides are all male. I see two of them. They have beards and they are 50-70 years old. It's Michael and Raphael (Archangels). Michael has blue eyes and their energy is similar. They say they are so glad to see me. They are celebrating to have me back.

P: They talk to me about Amber's life. They don't think I followed my path in that life. I needed to feel how the family felt. The guides explain that my role was to feel what it was like to live in that grey space where Tom and the boys lived. It is okay now, they tell me.

L: Where are we going next? Where are you?

P: I am now reviewing my goals. I am clearing out the emotions. It is like a cleanse. They are physically touching me. They are sending healing light to me. My guides tell me my greatest achievement was my spirituality after I left Tom and the boys. They are disappointed that I could not help the boys or Tom. They sucked my light and I lost energy. Tom dimmed my light.

P: My guides are showing me that when we first met, Tom and Amber, he was helping Indians and the white man. When he wasn't needed any more, his head became unhealthy. He felt so sorry for himself. There was nothing I could do, they say. He was sick. He started losing his sanity.

P: Then the boys followed him. It poisoned them. I just felt the disconnect. But, I didn't fully understand what was happening. I just felt the abandonment.

P: Archangels Michael and Raphael are telling me that the flow of the light is the energy that I run through my body. The light is the Christ Consciousness. It is the conductor of energy. They teach me how to work with it in each life. My pathway in this life on Earth comes from the planet I call home. I float outside the planet Urabitzia. This planet is in the same galaxy as Earth. There is a lot of water on Urabitzia. It is not a physical place we meet anymore. But outside the planet, we meet and my guides help me pull energy from Urabitzia to start my new lives each time.

L: Where are you moving to next? Is it the Council of Elders?

P: I am now moving to my Council of Elders. It's a big marble room. There are white column pillars. It's now enclosed, but open all around. There are five Elders. One is the leader. He looks like Abe Lincoln. Another one is female and she has on a goddess-like dress. The dress is gold and there is a medallion around her waist. It's clear with an aqua crystal in the center of the medallion. The three others are all in white gowns. Then I see Archangels Michael and Raphael to my left behind me. They are very pleased with me. Yet, they want me to go back out. The Goddess Elder says to me that I can see things in the crystal. She also has a scepter that is gold. She is showing me clouds and Earth. I am going back...

P: The Elders tell me that I need to use my energy to teach, talk and heal. I am not to worry about anyone around me and what I say to them. I do not decide. It's already mapped out for me. I am being handed a rock and I put it into my solar plexus. I absorb it. It is for just this present life I am living as Pamela. I am not the only one that is there. I see Mike and the girls (Priscilla has four daughters). They are being handed a rock as well and I am being told to go ahead.

L: What does the Council say the rock does for you?

P: The rock is what helps me to be human. It helps for me to have an easier transition to Earth. It is the size of an almond. It has to sit within me for a while. Then I go inside the rock itself. My spirit goes within the rock. Not until I do this am I able to put myself in the Earth life. Now I am getting close to coming into the womb for this present life. Now I feel myself inside the rock. It feels like a light egg. I am feeling the sensation of being inside the rock! The Council feels I could be moving faster. Once I get into the physical world and being on Earth, I get sidetracked.

L: What else does the Council want you to know?

P: The Council of Elders tells me I need to revert to my light form instead of the physical. They mean I need to be balancing my lightbody and my physical body. There is a way to do this and they are telling me I have done this before. I now need to move back into the lightbody more. I have done a good job with the girls. I need to move back into the light more. Mike, with his sense of humor, holds me back. He keeps me from talking about our light. They tell me that my parents are also from the same planet.

L: What percentage of your energy do you have on Earth?

P: The Council tells me that 80% of my energy I have brought to my human body. This is a characteristic that I carry. I heal others from the knowledge that I carry from my lightbody. My Council says that I need to learn to grow herbs again. It is energy that carries light on Earth that people can use.

L: What do you feel was your most significant life?

P: The Egyptian life. For Mike and me both, we accomplished so much in that life to help others.

L: What is the first life you remember in your higher consciousness?

P: During the dinosaur era, I was an animal. I was four-legged and I was smaller than a dinosaur. I was similar to an elephant but longer neck, thick and heavy. My first human life was very primitive like a cave man. I see that I have not been to Earth that often.

L: Are you in any special training groups when you are between lives and in spirit only?

Special training groups are formed by pulling away from your soul group with whom you have been connected for lifetime after lifetime. These special groups might be formed to teach souls special skills, such as learning to create matter, like rocks, grass, or trees. These special training groups may go to distant planets not yet developed, for beings to practice their skills on primitive, newly-formed planets, for example.

P: I reprogram energy for others. I have to talk to souls. I help reprogram and I also see that I was helped to be reprogrammed when I had returned to spirit from difficult lives.

P: This area we return to is dark initially. I work with really damaged souls. I shower them with light. They need debriefing. These souls have taken a wrong path in their previous life. Many times these souls stay in isolation for 4 or 5 Earth years. They were damaged to the point of being evil. Once they leave me, they go somewhere else. They might be being prepared to come back into human lives that are the exact opposite of the life they just experienced, to complete the karmic cycle of understanding.

L: Finally, Priscilla, what life or lives caused the feeling of abandonment to most set in?

P: It was the life when the house was burning with my two boys and my husband inside. Archangels Michael and Raphael are telling me they will help me release that feeling of anxiety and abandonment.

I visited with Priscilla weeks later, and she was feeling lighter and happier in her life today. She has begun a new job in computer technology for which Priscilla has a master's degree. When we see each other, we have an unspoken second language due to our experience together of her spiritual soul regression. This case was so unusual because it involved her husband, Mike, as her partner in most of her past lives. Plus, her daughters and parents were also repeatedly in most of her past lives. The entire group was from the distant planet, Urabitzia, and was sent here to Earth to help it progress to this most important shift we are experiencing now. They are here to bring love and light to all whom they touch in their lives.

Jayme Morgan made an appointment for a between lives regression in July of 2012. She told me how she was very much aligned with helping others. It gave her a mission for her life. She is a physical therapist by profession, had just moved to Colorado Springs, and hoped to connect with groups in volunteering her time to help others. She was also very interested in shamanism, having already participated in one year of intensive shamanic training. She felt that connecting to her higher soul self and her life's purpose by experiencing a between lives regression would help her clarify the many questions she had about her life.

Our session began as I moved her through past memories in this current life. We reached the period where she experienced her soul connecting with the physical body in the womb. She felt that it was a good match and that the body was very healthy. Jayme is a woman in her fifties today, and looks to be very healthy and fit. Next we regressed to her most recent life before the present one.

L: Can you tell me if you feel it's day or night, and are you inside a structure or outside in the open?

J: I am outside. I see blue sky and clouds. I also see trees and a meadow ahead. I am standing at the top of the meadow looking down into it below.

L: Look down at yourself and tell me what you are wearing.

J: I have on beaten-up leather shoes. I have on pants, but a long skirt over them. I have a blue shawl on over my clothes. It is all very simple dress.

L: What year do you see you are in and what is your name?

J: The year is 1876 and my name is the same, Jayme. I am 38 years old. I have a water bucket and I am walking to a house. The house is also very simple. I am at the front porch and now I am going inside. I see a fireplace that is smoking. I go over to warm my hands. I am now pouring the water from the bucket into a big pot over the fire. I am making soup. I see that I have one place setting. I had a breakup with a man. He went off on a hunting trip. I keep hoping that he will come back. His name is Jeff.

L: Do you recognize his soul essence as anyone you know in your current life?

J: Yes, he feels like my daughter's father, Bob.

L: Would you go to your parents in this past life and look at their soul essences? Do you recognize either your mother or your father as anyone you know in your current life as Jayme?

J: Yes, I see that my mother in this past life is the soul essence of my sister today and my father in this past life is my father today as well. In this past life in 1876, they have already passed. I see that I have a dog, Charlie, who is the soul essence of my dog today, Polly. They even look very similar. Polly is a border collie mix, and Charlie is a similar dog, and both are black and white.

J: I see that I have a lovely garden. I take care of it myself.
       I go to town to sell butter. I also knit and sell what I
       make. I see a loom in the corner of the room.

L: I want to move to the next most important scene in this
       past life you are experiencing on the count of three.
       One, two, and three.

J: I am sitting in my rocker. I am seventy years old. I just
       have my animals. I see chickens and roosters. There is
       no man. I feel sad. "Is this all there is?" I say to myself.
       I realize that I should have moved to town in this life to
       be around people and not so far out by myself.

L: Let's move to the last day of your life in this past life on
       the count of three. One, two, three.

J: I see that a young lady has come to help me. I'm dying.
       She says she will take care of the farm and animals. She
       just befriended me and really enjoyed being with me in
       my later years. Her name is Karen and she is crying as
       she is comforting me. I have now died.

J: I see her tidying up and stroking my hair after I have
       passed. (Jayme later told me the soul essence of Karen
       is her daughter in her present life.)

L: Before we leave this life, is there anyone you would like
       to say goodbye to, to put closure to this life?

J: Yes, I would like to go to Jeff. I wish you had let me know
       if you were dead or alive. Jeff is here and he is saying he
       tried, but I wasn't listening. He tried to connect to me
       from the spirit side many times, but I was always busy

with the animals and I didn't hear him. He says he died at twenty four.

L: Now as you rise up above your body, I want you to lift your soul self up higher and higher. Move up above the clouds, and now up into the outer atmosphere. You are feeling renewed energy now as you move into your true higher soul self.

J: I see the corona of the Earth. I am attracted to a star. It's a shining star. I feel like I am going home. I feel free of my body. The space is dark but the star is getting closer and brighter. I see bands of color, rainbow colors. Earth is tiny now. I feel the warmth of the star. It is Pleiades. It's pulling me in and wrapping me in a cocoon. It feels like a lily that hasn't opened yet. I am drawn into this bright light. Now beings greet me. They are bands of light. They are wrapping beams of light around me.

L: How many soul members do you see?

J: It's a collective group.   There is no clear definition of each soul.   They tell me that they see no need to separate. They are all the same size. They are beautiful bands of light. It seems so natural for them to be this way. I would say there are twelve or so souls.

J: I now see that Jesus joins us. He calls me beloved. He says we have much hope for you and your planet (Earth). We welcome you back here. They tell me my time is not done yet in my current life. They say they always want me to remember who I am. The soul group says that I always seem to forget. "Stay with us so you can heal," they say.

J: My father is one of the beams. My mother is, too. My brother James, my brother, Maney, and I see a little baby. I had an abortion when I was young. I also see my maternal grandmother as one of the beams, as well as my great aunt, my paternal grandmother, my cousin, John, and my Uncle Steve. I even see Monica, my friend, and a playmate from school, Nora, is also one of the beams. I see Kaye, whom I worked with in the past, is also one of the beams.

L: Is there anyone else here with you besides your soul group from Pleiades?

J: Yes, I see my master guide. He has the traditional flowing robe and a beard. He is about sixty years old. His name is Jim. He has beautiful blue eyes. They are piercing, but soft. He is tall, slender and smells good. He has long white hair in a pony tail. He is kind and very demonstrative. He is affectionate, yet very respectful of the feminine. He has good manners.

L: What does he tell you about the past life you just experienced?

J: He understands my sadness. He wishes I had sought out more people. He is reminding me that this past life wasn't bad. I enjoyed nature and not having to be with large groups of people. It was such a blessing that I was so kind to the animals. I asked Jim who the cow was. He says it was a sacred cow. One who was brought into my life to comfort me.

L: Where are you being taken now?

J: We are walking down a dirt road that looks like Florida. I am having the memory of my brother, Maney, who died two years ago. Jim is saying that this has nothing to do with Maney. This is just a dusty road. It's always led you back home. You were never apart from us. It doesn't matter what the road looks like. We are always here for you. You are never alone.

J: I am now being shown the Mediterranean. I am being shown the Adriatic Sea. It is a beautiful scene. This is the water from where I came. My guide, Jim, is saying it sparkles just as I do. There is some sort of underground community below the water. It is where I once lived. The nation is called Nivia. It is no longer on Earth. It was before Lemuria. It is before 15,000 years ago. It was the beginning of great things to come, such as Lemuria. Nivia existed probably 100,000 years ago. My daughter, Ellen, was there with me. My mother was, too. I could shape shift. I could be like a human and then turn into a mermaid with one thick trunk and fishtail. I had long hair. I was beautiful. I lived on land and water both. I was held in high regard in our domain. I was one of the few who could go back and forth between two legs and a fish tail. Many of our people were fighting to become two-legged. The others were feeling the separation of the change. They held fear and did not trust the new life as a two-legged.

L: Where do you want to go to next?

J: I feel like I am at the Grand Canyon and I'm on a cliff looking down. I see flat rocks. My guide, Jim, is telling me it's to gain perspective. And this location reminds me of where the Essenes lived. The sun is gorgeous and I am gathering strength from it. I am being nourished by it. Now he is showing me a beautiful eagle. The eagle is to remind me of my keen sight. I do have the wings to fly above all obstacles.

L: Where are you being taken now?

J: I am with my Council of Elders. I am feeling caution. They are a group of women. They know me. I am ready to receive them. There are thirteen of them. The Chairman is Mary Anne. She has on a long skirt to the ground and she is dressed like a Native American. She wears a band of feathers in her hair off to one side. She has on a lot of turquoise. She is handing me a pipe. I see that it has a stick figure drawing on the pipe. It's a smoking pipe. Another elder is African-looking. She is wearing a row of beads around her neck. She has dark skin. She says, "I am Yohanna, honey." Her left arm is covered in bangles. She is holding a basket and is offering it to me. It has dead lizards in it for ceremonies. I take it.

J: I am ready to listen. Jim is standing behind me. The scene looks like New Mexico. I see lots of red rock. A big fire is going. We are all sitting down around the fire. I have the pipe and I am being honored. Now I am passing it around.

J: Mary Anne speaks and asks me why I am afraid of loving myself. I thought I was getting better. Mary Anne says that I hold back. She says I have immeasurable worth. It's time to open up and I must do that now. I know it's a fear of rejection. I am not knowing and remembering who I am; what a perfect being that I am. The elders say I forget this and put up very big shields. They have an openness, but they are adamant that I clear this fear so that I can do the work this time in my present life.

L: Can they tell you any more about your current life's path?

J: They say I must proceed. I am on course. They don't
       have to push me. I am pushing myself. The main goal
       is to get beyond the fear of rejection. Try to remember
       and bring back all my strong experiences in past lives.
       It's time to release any fears you have had from these
       hard lives, they tell me. There is no reason I can't be
       who I am, which is strong and truthful. The Council of
       Elders say that in order to do that, I must branch out
       more. I need to find like-minded people. I need to make
       more connections to meet and develop relationships.

L: One of Jayme's questions for me to ask the Council of
       Elders was about her relationships in this present life.
       Do they speak of any men in your future?

J: I am going to be very busy. I will meet someone through
       my group involvement. By meeting this man, it will
       open up a part of me that is not asking for just fun, but
       a deep, lasting relationship.

L: What was your most significant past life?

J: My past life as Ocala, a Native American. I have mainly
       lived as a woman. They are showing me that many lives
       have been indigenous lives and some around mountains.
       Pleiades was before Earth. It is my origin. The middle
       earth life in water about 100,000 years ago in Nivia was
       my first Earth life.

L: What does the Council of Elders tell you was your most
       productive life?

J: The life as Ocala. I was a Medicine Woman. I had direct
       connection to source. I would help other people to heal
       and connect themselves to source very successfully.

The Council says that, of course, I can repeat this very successful life in my present life.

J: We have left the campfire and I am on a horse now. They are telling me that if I explore other geographical locations such as Garden of the Gods, they will give me more information about those areas while in the Akashic Records. (Jayme later told me she visits the Akashic Records when she is in a dream state as she sleeps.) I will be able to benefit the Earth by receiving their wisdom and knowledge received in the Records.

L: Tell me how you decide on your next life when you are in spirit.

J: There are several things to choose from. A lot of my soul family will gather around and remind me of things I have learned and what I have decided I want to work on for the future. But ultimately, it's my decision. We look at the goals and then the body is looked at also. We look at the genetic make-up, the health, and so on of the human body before deciding on the best one for me.

L: How did these goals help you to decide on your present life as Jayme?

J: The choices I made had a lot to do with my parents. I selected a father who traveled, and a mother who was nurturing so that I could explore my world in a protective environment.

L: Do you put your soul self in scenes before selecting the life in order to understand firsthand the life you are about to select?

J: Yes, I do sometimes. But due to free will, it is always
      a gamble even if you know the parents from previous
      lives.

L: How much of your total energy from your higher self
      did you bring into this present life?

J: I use between 40% and 65% of my total higher soul self
      energy, depending on what is needed for the circum-
      stances. It would take effort, but I could bring in more
      than 65% if the occasion called for it.

L: What does Jim, your master guide, tell you your mission
      is in your present life?

J: Jim says to share the love with everyone. He shows me
      that I have light that emanates from me. He says to just
      be the light in the room. That is my path in this life.

L: One of the questions you had for your master guide,
      Jim, was concerning your daughter, Ellen. Ask Jim why
      Ellen has been such a problematic teenager and adult.

J: Jim says that she is here to help me stand strong and
      build fortitude. She is to help me recognize that her
      decisions are very different than mine.

As Jayme ended the session and sat up on the sofa to
regroup from the between lives regression, she remembered
the lunch she had had that day with her co-workers. They were
discussing a new program on television about mermaids.
Scientists are finding evidence that there may have been a
civilization that once had long tails and fins like mermaids
who lived on Earth centuries ago. When her friends scoffed
at the idea, Jayme defended the idea and instead found it

very interesting. She realized, from her instant reaction, all her life she had been attracted to any subject matter to do with mermaids. Now, from what she had experienced in the between lives regression, she understood why. It triggered an old life that had been very precious to her for her strength and accommodation.

The message from all the sessions with the light beings is always the same. We are all here to spread the light and the love, to lift up each other, and to help the vibration of Earth ascend to a higher human consciousness. Sometimes, it's not to lead a healing or spiritual life. It is just to be. When we act from the heart, we lift each other to a higher plane.

Jayme, like so many of the advanced light beings that are here on Earth at this time, is to hold the light for everyone she comes in contact with. Jayme's soul has been coming to earth for thousands of years, bringing our evolution from a mermaid-type being to a two-legged human, and then continuing in time as a human to help evolve the human species to this very time of the great shift. We are blessed that so many beings want to help us and our planet Earth move into a higher vibration of the 5th dimension.

CHAPTER FOURTEEN
A Progressive Life on Venus

Hanna Wittmier came to me for a past life regression as I was writing this book. At first I thought against adding it, as unusual as it was. After all, my book was at the editor's and it was complete. But something, meaning my spirit guides, kept intuitively telling me Hanna's story needed to be in this book.

Hanna called me to set up a typical appointment for a past life regression session. When we met, her needs for the regression seemed fairly common. She felt she had fears that were holding her back in life. She felt that every time she tried to move forward, she would be stopped by her fears. Secondly, she felt that she did not use her voice. She said she let people roll all over her. She expressed that she had had many traumas in her present life. She had lost her husband to an aorta dissection at his heart. She herself had had a brain tumor which had been successfully removed.

As we entered into the first scene, I immediately knew we were not on Earth. The rest continued to amaze me because Hanna showed all the signs of actual suffering in her facial expressions and her breathing patterns. Her breathing during the entire regression was labored and intense. Her facial expressions were of extreme sorrow. So now let's begin.

L: Does it appear to be day or night to you, Hanna?

H: It is day and I am outside.

L: How are you feeling? (I could see that she was stressed.)

H: I am frustrated. I feel an overwhelming sadness. I am tired. I also feel very tense. My mouth and chin feel sore. I feel so much tension, that I have made my jaw sore. I need to let go of the tenseness.

L: Where are you? What are the surrounding scenes that you see?

H: I am in a cave. I see different colors. My head hurts. I see shadowy objects. I feel the energy of other people, even though I can't actually see them. The other people look shadowy and grey. I am hiding in the cave. Something wants to hurt me. My head hurts. I am not the only one hiding. The other shadowy figures are here, too. I can't breathe.

L: Tell me about yourself. What do you look like, and are you male or female?

H: We are not people. We are more like spirit.

L: So you are a form of spirit, not in a body form...

L: Where are you?

H: We are not on Earth.

L: Are you in the galaxy?

H: Yes.

L: Are you on the Moon, or are you on Mars, or Venus?

H: Not the Moon, and definitely not Mars. We are on Venus.

L: What is happening to you on Venus? You are obviously under some kind of immense stress. (Hanna was grimacing and straining in her facial expressions as she spoke to me under trance.)

H: Chemicals. Someone brought them. The chemicals will kill us. We just have a few hours left to survive. The taste in my mouth is bitter from the chemicals. We can't help but breathe the chemicals in. I am feeling dizzy. I see myself sitting down. I am trying to stand up, but I cannot. I am white light that has a shadowy shape. I am looking for someone. I am looking for a child. I see that all the shadowy figures are dead. They are all dead. All the other people around me are dead now. I can feel them around me.

L: Do you recognize the soul essence of any of the people as anyone you know today in your life as Hanna?

H: Yes. I see my son, Donnie, as one of the people. And I also see my mom, Kathy, as one of them. I feel tense. Earth brought these chemicals. The inhabitants of Earth brought the chemicals to kill everyone here.

L: So it is Earth that has caused this destruction. The Earth inhabitants are trying to destroy any life on Venus.

L: Can you tell me the year?

H: It is the future. The year is 2025.

L: Please tell me what happens to you next.

H: I am still alive. Somehow, I am still alive. There are
      some others that are still alive. We have been here
      about a week. I eat plants. We have no food. We are
      dying.

L: What happens next?

H: I have died. I see no other shadowy figures. We are all
      gone.

L: Please let your spirit rise above your shadowy form
      and float up above the scene and up above the planet.
      Now you are residing in a higher vibrational level. Here
      you are now residing with your spirit guides, and any
      ascended beings that guide you. I want you to ask them
      to come through now and answer our questions about
      the life you just saw in the future on the count of three.
      One, two, three.

H: I feel a loving feeling all around me. It is feminine in
      nature. She is Alondra. She is my master guide. There
      is also a male guide here. His name is Michael.

L: Is there anyone else here with us today?

H: Yes, there is a child. His name is Steven. He is very
      joyful.

L: Thank you Alondra and Michael and Steven for being
      with us today. Can you tell us more about why you
      showed Hanna this future life? Is this life simultaneously
      going on as Hanna is experiencing her own life?

H: We want her to take care of herself. She feels so much
      fear. The fear is from the life she is experiencing on

Venus. She knows her fate and is worrying so about it. We also want to tell her to drink more water. Water is very important. We are sending her downloads of light and she must drink lots of water to cleanse the toxins out of her body now. She worries too much for this future life and it is compromising her present life as Hanna.

H: Yes, it is a parallel life, my guides say.

L: What can Hanna do for her headaches? She experienced headaches on Venus, and now she also experiences many headaches in her life as Hanna.

H: My guides say that I have to move. The elevation is too high for me here. My body needs more moisture. It's too dry here. Maine, Minnesota or even Arizona elevation would be much better for me to rid myself of the headaches. They are telling me to be brave. I am to keep doing what I am doing. Sharing the light. I am being downloaded with light to pass on to others on Earth.

L: Can your guides tell us how to relieve your fears?

H: These fears keep me stuck, they say. Some of the fear is coming from this parallel life, but not all of it. My guides say I am not ready to deal with all the fear. Some of it is from other past lives. Someone murdered me in a past life. It is the soul essence of my father in this present life as Hanna...

H: I am slow to learn, Alondra says. I am stubborn. I have asked for really hard lessons to grow my soul. I asked for no lies. They tell me my father's soul asked for the murder to happen for his soul growth, and I agreed. Alondra and Michael say that I can stop now with the hard lessons. The trauma of the hard lessons has set up too many fears that I now have to face to move on. My spirit guides tell me that speaking the truth got me killed.

L: We now ask that the White Brotherhood, my spirit guides, bring Hanna light to her heart chakra to let the fear go. I ask that you bring this light also to Hanna's throat chakra. This will allow her not to fear speaking for herself in the future. I ask for Hanna and me to take a deep breath as the light is sent to her throat and heart.

H: I see that men I have chosen in my present life have been bad men. I can now speak from my heart. I have always been honest. I need to now be honest with myself. I need to stop denying my intuitive reading of human spirit. I know the inner feelings of people who are close to me. I need to start relying on that feeling.

H: This place is hard for Donnie. He doesn't understand the hard, dark energy sometimes experienced on Earth. Alondra is telling me, "Just ask his guides to surround him," when he is troubled.

L: Any final words from your guides?

H: "Keep doing what you are doing on Earth."

We have just experienced a future life session. This was a very interesting case for me. I feel I will be dealing with many more of these cases in the future as our veil regarding higher vibrations becomes thinner and thinner. We are now able to accept the possibility of parallel lives, future lives and more. We are ready for this understanding and I feel it is an exciting time in our history for these discoveries in regressive therapy work.

As we ended the session and Hanna had time to reflect on the session she had just had, she had some observations. Hanna told me that several times in dreams and other visions, she had repeatedly been shown a life where there were big animals all around her. They looked similar to our dinosaurs but smaller in size. Could these have been in the parallel life on Venus?

The fear and dread she always felt was mainly from this parallel life where she intuitively knew she was going to end her life badly. But part of the fear was from a past life she was not even ready to see. I always tell everyone before a session not to fear anything you will see, and that you will only be shown a life or a scene that you are prepared to see. Here is proof that that is true. Hanna is not ready to see a life that is still bringing her fear today when she was murdered for speaking her truth.

By helping her release some of her fear by viewing the parallel life and also surrounding her in white light to open her throat and heart chakras, Hanna should be more at peace in the future.

Hanna is a woman of about 40 years of age. She will probably live to the year of 2060 or beyond. This is well beyond the end of her parallel shadowy figure life on Venus where she died in 2025. That seems like a very short time from now that Earth would be traveling to Venus to send out chemicals to end life there. I ask you to read this material with an open mind, but to be open to many causes of our human soul's experience of pain and suffering. It may not be what you think. Hanna's story is a good case for not judging another soul's path because we do not know what shoes they walk in.

Epilogue

I will be writing more in the future concerning compelling sessions of past life regression and between lives regression work. These preceding chapters were chosen specifically to help you, the reader, to open your mind in looking at different ways souls come to Earth. I also hope I have brought some regressions that will help others to identify their phobias, ailments, or anxieties that might be caused by past life trauma.

Most importantly, I hope the burning desire I have to do this work will spread to others to use it for more mainstream problems. Many times people come to me for readings for the present. It is not unusual that during the reading, I get a strong nudge from my spirit guides that their problems are from trauma from a past life or lives. I quickly tell them they can be helped by delving into a past life regression to get more information on why they react the way they do to certain events or relationships. Many take my advice while others choose to continue to be clouded by events.

Our spirit guides are just on the other side of the veil (which is thinning daily). They vibrate at a different rate, so they seem invisible to us, but they are always around us and want to help us on our unique journeys on earth, whatever they may be. When each person relaxes to an alpha or theta brain wave state, they are able to see an important past life or between lives soul state through their subconscious mind. In addition, just as important, they are able to connect to their spirit guides. This relationship may have already been established for some individuals previous to the regression, but I guarantee that you will connect on a new, deeper level during your past life regression or between lives regression experience. This will open the door to a future of better and deeper connection to your guides that you can enjoy for the rest of your life.

The spirit guides would like nothing more than to be your guide on your journey. They are here to help you with intuitive decisions for your life. They will never give you answers, they will just lead you to the crossroads, and it is up to you to decide which road to take. We humans must physically do the work, but our spirit guides can help us discover the steps to achieving our goals.

You have just read some pretty incredible regression stories. I would ask that you suspend your judgment for a moment and let the book and its contents resonate for a while with you before you decide how you feel about the information. We cannot see the light waves of our computer, yet we trust the information we are receiving. We get our communication on smart phones from satellites in the upper atmosphere that we cannot see or feel, yet we trust the voice at the other end that we are having a conversation with. And just as easily, these light beings have entered our atmosphere to share in the experience of being human to raise up the future of our planet Gaia.

As you have read, most advanced beings come in peace and harmony and bring with them the light to lift us all up. There are dark forces on the planet as well, but, to my knowledge, I have never been affected in any way by the darkness. I always surround myself with beautiful, golden light that I call the Christ Consciousness light before I start any facilitation. And I ask for the protection of Jeshua or Archangel Michael before I start my work each day.

The message continues to be that we must work in groups to share our strengths for the planet. All the damage that humans have done to our air, water, and food sources has put our Mother Earth terribly out of balance. New forms of clean energy, organic plant-based non-genetically-modified food sources, and cleaner water will not only help humans to survive into the new century, but will help species that are daily leaving this planet to stay longer without going extinct. I was reading recently that research is estimating that many bees will be extinct in 30 years and some of our food sources will dry up because of lack of fertilization by bees. We cannot allow this to happen in this lifetime. This is just one example of how we are not using enough natural products to reproduce food sources.

We humans can turn this around by using more renewable products without harmful pesticides or chemicals. If we all work together, putting each person's skill to work in whatever capacity they have, we can achieve a common goal of restoring our planet to its healthy form. Saving planet Earth is important not only to humans, but to many advanced civilizations in other solar systems and from other galaxies, as we have heard in the past life regressions and between life regressions recounted in this book. What happens to Earth affects many other civilizations beyond our small third rock from the sun.

Please know that my spirit guides have told me many, many times that all we do each day makes a difference. When I ask if my work is helping to be of service to the planet, my guides always give me the same answer. They say everything we do helps. Everything we do, each and every day helps. Love and light to you.

> We are the miracle of force and matter
> making itself over into imagination and will.
> Incredible. The life Force experimenting
> with forms. You are one. Me for another. The
> Universe has shouted itself alive. We are one
> of the shouts. [16]

---

[16] Ray Bradbury, *I Sing the Body Electric: And Other Stories* (New York, New York: HarperCollins Publishers, Inc. Avon Books, 1998), 12.

Bibliography

Backman, Ph. D, Linda. *Bringing Your Soul to Light: Healing through Past lives and the Time Between.* Woodbury, Minnesota: Llewellyn Worldwide Ltd., 2009.

Bradbury, Ray. *I Sing the Body Electric: And Other Stories,* New York, New York: HarperCollins Publishers, Inc., Avon Books, 1998.

Cannon, Dolores. *The Convoluted Universe, Book IV.* Huntsville, Arkansas: Ozark Mountain Publishing, 2012.

Chodron, Pema. *When Things Fall Apart, Heart Advice for Difficult Times.* Massachusetts: Shambala Publishing, Inc., 1997.

Cori, Patricia. *The Starseed Dialogues, Soul Searching the Universe.* Berkeley, California: North Atlantic Books, 2009.

McHugh CCHt, Greg. *The New Regression Therapy, Healing the Wounds and Trauma of This Life and Past Lives With the Presence and the Light of the Divine.* Denver, Colorado: Greg McHugh, 2010.

Murray, Fiona. *Elemental Beings.* http:// www.elementalbeings.co.uk., May, 2012.

Newton, PhD, Michael. *Life Between Lives, Hypnotherapy for Spiritual Regression.* Minnesota: Llewellyn Worldwide, Ltd., 2009.

Roberts, Jane. *Psychic Politics.* New Jersey: Prentice-Hall Publishing, 1976.

Saint Ignatius of Loyola and Mottola, Anthony,(Jan. 7, 1964), *Spiritual Exercises of Saint Ignatius,* New York, New York: Doubleday div. of Bantam Doubleday Dell Publishing Group Inc, 1964.

Semkiw, MD, Walter. *Born Again, Reincarnation Cases Involving International Celebrities, India's Political Legends and Film Stars.* New Delhi, India: Ritana Books, Defense Colony Flyover Market, 2006.

Sutphen, Richard. *You Were Born Again To Be Together.* Charlottesville, Virginia: Hampton Roads Publishing Co. Inc., 1976.

Tachi-ren, Tashira. *What Is Lightbody, Archangel Ariel Channeled by Tashira Tachi-ren.* Lithia Springs, Georgia: World Tree Press, 1990, 1999, 2007.

Young, Meredith Lady. *Agartha,* Walpole, New Hampshire: Stillpoint Publishing, 1984.

We Are the Ones We Have Been Waiting For, The Hopi Elders Speak, Attributed to anUnnamed Hopi Elder, Hopi Nation, Oraibi, Arizona

ABOUT THE AUTHOR

Lee Mitchell graduated with a business degree and minor in psychology from North Texas State University (University of Texas at Denton). Lee had a career in real estate that spanned over 30 years with the last ten being her own general contracting business, Lee Mitchell Homes, Inc., in Crestone and Salida, Colorado. Though Lee had always been intrigued with Dr. Michael Newton's studies on past life and between life regression work, and had attended a workshop with Dr. Brian Weiss, it was not until 2007 that she made the move to become certified as a past life regression hypnotherapist. She was certified by Linda Backman, PhD. whom had trained with Dr. Michael Newton and had been one of his original instructors for the past life and between life regression academy he founded in Arizona.

Presently, Lee has regressed almost one thousand clients either in groups or individually. Lee works out of Denver and Colorado Springs, Colorado, Cheyenne, Wyoming, and Sarasota, Florida. Soon to start facilitating in San Diego, California, she has expanded her work to include attachment release. Lee Mitchell originates from Denton, Texas where much of her family still lives including a sister and brother and their families. Lee lives in Littleton, Colorado with her only child, Casey, her walker hound whom has her own healing abilities. Lee is also a spiritual intuitive and has a lively practice reading for others in her home, and in metaphysical stores in the Denver and Colorado Springs area.

Visit her website at: www.crystalsoulpath.com